Black Cat Raiders

of WW II

BLACK CAT RAIDERS

of WW II

Richard C. Knott

The Nautical & Aviation Publishing Company of America
Annapolis, Maryland

Library of Congress Catalog Card Number 81-11352
ISBN 0-933852-18-5
Printed in the United States of America.

PBYs were patrol aircraft—slow, cumbersome, and vulnerable to fighter attack. (U.S. Navy)

To Eleanor

Contents

Introduction

This is a story of war and vengeance in the South Pacific, of courage in the face of overwhelming odds, and of the unlikely phoenix bird that rose from the ashes of defeat to repay its tormentors—in spades. The story is true, pieced together from a variety of sources including war diaries, squadron histories, reports of action against the enemy, message traffic, official and personal correspondence, and other documents. The names used are those of real persons, many of whom are still living and some of whom have contributed their recollections to this account.

When the war erupted in 1941, the U.S. Navy's PBY flying boats were already obsolescent. The British had named them Catalinas, after the idyllic island off the California coast; the Americans, with their penchant for abbreviating everything, inevitably called them Cats. But they were more like sitting ducks to the Japanese fighter pilots who ruled the air in the Western Pacific during the early months of the war. The Cats were no match for the swift and deadly Zeros, and although they engaged the enemy as best they could, the outcome of these encounters was rarely cause for celebration. Sometimes a battered Cat managed to slip away to fight again, but the grim toll of losses was sobering.

By mid-1942, attention was focused on the fact that the few PBY combat missions which could be called successful had almost invariably been flown at night. This realization led to the idea that turned selected PBY squadrons into deadly hunters. The first step in the transformation was a coat of flat black paint, followed by installation of exhaust flame arresters and by a fundamental change in operating procedure. The Cats would sleep by day and prowl at night. Airborne radar developed by the British enabled them to see in the dark. Their revolutionary new radar capability, coupled with their sinister appearance and nocturnal habits, gave them an almost supernatural aura. The Black Cats soon became legend throughout the Southwest Pacific.

To the Japanese the Cats seemed to appear out of nowhere, pouncing upon fleet units and cargo vessels. Attacks were typically made from 2,000 feet in a shallow dive, with engines throttled back to a whisper. By the time the Cats were detected at masthead level by a startled lookout or an unwary officer of the deck, it was too late.

Of course the initial attack rarely resulted in an immediate kill. More often than not, the Cats were obliged to return to the target more than once. On these subsequent passes a fully alerted enemy was ready with a lethal antiaircraft barrage. The ensuing duels between aircraft and ship were sometimes fierce and bloody. Cats often returned to base riddled by machine gun fire, with gaping holes in their wings.

The Black Cats accounted for the sinking or disabling of several hundred thousand tons of Japanese cargo vessels, troop transports, and warships. Curiously, however, their exploits are not widely known today, except to a few aviation history buffs and those surviving pilots and crewmen who took part in their operations. Although they established for themselves an enviable reputation for skill and daring, their operations were not the kind which ordinarily captured the headlines at home. A typical Black Cat began its mission at dusk from an island base or a tender in some isolated lagoon, spent hours searching for its prey and, finding it, fought its grim battle alone in the dark, aircraft-against-ship to a final conclusion. When morning came, only an oil slick might remain as mute testimony to the struggle.

This book is a tribute to those who kept the faith when hope was lost, and to others who came afterward and blazed a trail of burning ships from the Solomons to the Philippines. It is the saga of the flying felines of World War II who came to be known as *The Black Cats*.

Black
Cat
Raiders
of WW II

A Taste of Defeat

He had been unable to shake that feeling of uneasiness ever since his arrival almost a year before. Like other senior aviators who had survived man's early investigations into the mysteries of powered flight, Pat Bellinger had developed a personal warning system, a kind of sixth sense triggered by seemingly insignificant things—the color of engine exhaust smoke, the flutter of a control surface, the changing sounds of air passing through struts and wires. Over the years this extrasensory mechanism had matured and become a part of his everyday life. Now it was again telling him that something was wrong.

With a half-frown he scrutinized the Catalina flying boats that squatted in the fading light like great seabirds come ashore to rest. To the casual eye they looked impressive, to some perhaps even formidable. But the solemn-faced man who stood alone on the parking apron knew their real capabilities and he had deep reservations. They were patrol aircraft, cumbersome and slow, designed primarily for long-range search. But because war has a habit of disregarding such orderly distinctions, they were armed with machine guns and were capable of carrying a respectable load of bombs or torpedoes slung under the wings. In the event of a shooting confrontation, could these middle-aged mammoths really be expected to attack an enemy warship or a fortified installation—and survive? Perhaps even more important, could they even defend themselves adequately against modern fighters? And if they could, would there be enough of them, and enough crews to fly them, to meet the challenge he thought might come, perhaps without warning?

His somber thoughts contrasted with the serene setting of the moment. A soft southwesterly breeze blew in from the sea and the sky had turned to a deep orange-red in the last moments before darkness. At the naval base just across the channel, lights began to wink on reassuringly while along the eastern side of Ford Island the outlines of the great battleships of the U.S. Pacific Fleet had begun to fade into the darkening sky. He could not see them from where he stood, but he knew they were there. One could almost feel their presence. They seemed to underscore the widely held view that an enemy attack on this island bastion would be an incomprehensible act of suicide by any aggressor. And the only plausible aggressor in this part of the world was more than three thousand miles to the west. Nevertheless, the feeling of uneasiness would not leave him.

Bellinger shrugged his shoulders in resignation. He did not like being thought an alarmist, and he suspected that he had already managed to raise too many eyebrows among his superiors in Washington. Still, it was he who bore a major share of the responsibility for the air defense of Pearl Harbor and he knew only too well that his ability to protect the great naval base was sadly deficient, in both material assets and trained personnel.

But Washington's interest seemed to be focused on the Atlantic where our old ally England was waist-deep in a war with Germany, and France had already fallen without much of a fight. German U-boats prowled the Atlantic with virtual impunity and President Franklin D. Roosevelt had ordered U.S. ships and aircraft to patrol the vast ocean approaches to the East Coast and Caribbean. Indeed, the President seemed preoccupied with the threat from Europe and only mildly concerned with the ominous storm signals emanating from the Far East. But perhaps this attitude was no more than a prudent politician's deference to public opinion.

There were too many Americans who believed that war with Japan could not be a serious consideration and they seemed bent on convincing others that obliviousness was the key to peace. To the various pacifist organizations in opposition to increased defense spending, war with Germany was to be scrupulously avoided—but war with Japan was unthinkable. There were, of course, Americans who understood clearly that the United States and Japan were drifting toward a head-on clash. But the domestic political climate was such that to speak out on this matter could be personally hazardous.

That facet of the problem was made clear to military men in particular when Rear Admiral Joseph K. Taussig was called by a Senate committee to testify on the need for a naval expansion program. Unfortunately for Taussig, he made the mistake of stating bluntly that the United States might one day find itself at war with Japan. His comments brought a

Pearl Harbor before the December 7 attack. The arrow marks the PATWING 2 hangar and ramp area on Ford Island. (U.S. Navy)

prompt disclaimer of responsibility from the State and Navy Departments and a call by Representative Hamilton Fish of New York for an investigation of warlike utterances by military men. Senator Clark of Missouri called Taussig's testimony disgraceful, and suggested that it might be a proper basis for a court-martial. Talk of war was simply not popular with Americans and they would hear none of it. Some of these same people would later clamor for the heads of "those responsible" for the inevitable disaster.[1]

Captain P. N. L. (Pat) Bellinger had arrived at Pearl Harbor in late 1940 to become Commander, Patrol Wing 2. Shortly after assuming command he was promoted to Rear Admiral. Bellinger had begun his flying career as naval aviator number eight in 1914; no naval officer

5

P.N.L. "Pat" Bellinger as a vice admiral. (U.S. Navy)

knew more about seaplane operations in general, and patrol aviation in particular.

Pat Bellinger saw immediately that the state of readiness was inadequate, and on January 16, 1941 fired off a letter through the chain of command to make his views known to Admiral Harold R. Stark, Chief of Naval Operations.

> I arrived here on October 30, 1940, with the point of view that the international situation was critical, especially in the Pacific, and I was impressed with the need of being ready today rather than tomorrow for any eventuality that might arise. After taking command of Patrol Wing Two and looking over the situation, I was surprised to find that here in the Hawaiian Islands, an important naval advanced outpost, we were operating on a shoestring and the more I looked the thinner the shoestring appeared to be.[2]

He went on to list in some detail what he considered to be the important "deficiencies and requirements" and prefaced this list with an ominous warning:

This letter is written merely in an effort to insure that we may not be "too late."[3]

Then he set about doing what he could, on his own, to be ready for the coming conflict.

About the first of March 1941 Bellinger met with Major General F. L. Martin, commander of U.S. Army Air Forces in Hawaii, to work out a joint plan for the air defense of the islands. Operational realities of the day dictated the tactics which could be expected from an enemy carrier force bent on making a surprise attack. Bellinger reasoned that such a force would be likely to approach its objective to within approximately 700 miles during the late afternoon or evening of the day preceding the strike. Then, under cover of night, it would steam at maximum speed so as to be within air range of the target area at dawn and launch its aircraft before being discovered. Consequently, if U.S. air patrols could locate the enemy on the afternoon or evening prior to the planned attack, this could provide maximum time to thwart the attack, or at least make defensive preparations. For an island like Pearl Harbor, patrols would be required to a distance of 700 miles in all directions, a formidable undertaking.

Bellinger's and Martin's plan, which turned out to be prophetic, reflected this reasoning and envisioned an air attack launched from enemy carriers operating within 300 miles of the islands. The plan prescribed daily long-distance patrols through 360 degrees to counter the threat. Unfortunately there were no aircraft available for the task. Organizationally speaking, Bellinger's PBYs were fleet aircraft and were heavily committed to training requirements decreed in Washington, meant to expand rapidly the number of trained patrol-plane crews. The few Army aircraft that might be made available in the event of a probable attack were unsuitable for the mission, in both numbers and capability. Bellinger had been given the title of Commander, Naval Base Defense Air Force, but as he later observed, this command was only a "paper" organization. "It did not exist until put into effect by proper orders."[4]

Meanwhile work continued on Johnson, Midway, Palmyra, and Wake Islands to get them ready for expanded seaplane operations. These projects involved the building of concrete ramps and parking aprons and often required the blasting of coral heads to a depth of six feet or more so that the PBYs could use the sheltered lagoons for basing. All this was time-consuming, but Bellinger kept prodding in an attempt to keep the work on schedule. Construction of the new naval air station at Kaneohe Bay on the eastern side of Oahu was still underway, and this was another matter of concern to him.

7

Readiness seemed constantly on Pat Bellinger's mind. During the early part of 1941 he decided it was time to see just how quickly his PBYs could react if called upon suddenly to take offensive action against the Japanese. One day without warning he ordered all aircraft loaded with live 500-pound bombs. These were not stored on Ford Island where the PBYs were based and had to be ferried from an ammunition dump by boat. Loading equipment was in short supply and because of the strenuous flight-training requirements, the crews had insufficient practice in handling live ordnance. Bellinger observed the loading operation, timing it carefully, and was appalled by the unsatisfactory results. He forwarded an official account of his findings to the Navy Department to dramatize his dilemma. For his trouble, he was told to dispense with live loading drills. Perhaps it was felt that the slow and highly vulnerable PBYs would never be called upon to engage in offensive action against a heavily armed opponent. Most likely, there were more pressing problems to deal with at higher levels and taken in the overall context of things, this problem seemed relatively insignificant.

As the year progressed, Bellinger put his squadrons on an expanded work schedule and by fall had ordered all of his aircraft to be fully armed with machine guns on all flights. By this time PBY squadrons of Patrol Wing 1 were based at the new naval air station at Kaneohe Bay and were also operating under Bellinger's overall command. New PBY-5s and PBY-5As had begun to arrive, with two full squadrons making their appearance on November 23, 1941. But Bellinger's time was running out. Even at this late date there were insufficient spare parts and other essential equipment, and the training schedule with its accompanying maintenance load continued to preclude the kind of regular and sustained long-distance patrols needed to provide adequate warning of an imminent attack. Perhaps most disturbing was the general perception of safety and security that had infected almost everyone on this island paradise. If war was to come, it would certainly not start here. It was this state of mind that caused Rear Admiral Pat Bellinger to linger that evening on the darkening seaplane ramp and perhaps to wonder if it might not be he who was out of step with the world. His answer would soon be forthcoming. Unknown to him, events were already unfolding which would ultimately confirm his worst fears.

On November 5, 1941, the Japanese Cabinet had met and given its approval for war with the United States. Admiral Isoroku Yamamoto, author of "Plan One," the original design to attack Pearl Harbor, ordered mission commander Vice Admiral Chuichi Nagumo to complete his preparations, and on the morning of the 26th the Japanese striking force departed remote Hitokappu Bay in the Kurile Islands and headed southeast toward Hawaii. A force of submarines, including several two-man midget submersibles riding piggyback on the larger vessels, had preceded the carrier force to congregate off the entrance to Pearl Harbor. At the appropriate time, the midgets were expected to penetrate harbor defenses and fire their torpedoes at suitable targets, causing as much damage and confusion among U.S. forces as possible.

Admiral Kimmel, Commander-in-Chief of the U.S. Pacific Fleet, had already been advised in a dispatch from the Chief of Naval Operations on the 24th that negotiations with the Japanese held little hope of success and that "a surprise aggressive movement in any direction including

Shown are .50-caliber waist guns trained aft. There was also a .30-caliber gun in the nose and another in the tunnel hatch beneath the aircraft. (U.S. Navy)

9

attack on Philippines or Guam is a possibility."[5] No mention was made in this communication, however, that an attack on Hawaii was even a remote consideration. On the 27th Kimmel received another more ominous message which read, in part:

> This dispatch is to be considered a war warning. Negotiations with Japan looking toward stabilization of conditions in the Pacific have ceased and an aggressive move by Japan is expected within the next few days. The number and equipment of Japanese troops and the organization of naval task forces indicates an amphibious expedition against either the Philippines, Thai or Kra Peninsula or possibly Borneo. Execute an appropriate defensive deployment preparatory to carrying out the tasks assigned.[6]

It was clear to the Pacific Fleet Commander that war was imminent, but this dispatch confirmed his previous understanding that an attack on Pearl Harbor could be ruled out. Unfortunately, it appears that other information available in Washington both prior and subsequent to the 27th, suggesting that Pearl Harbor might indeed be the target of the Japanese fleet, was somehow not relayed to the Army and Navy commanders in Hawaii. Under the circumstances, Kimmel did not feel it necessary to provide Bellinger with a copy of the ambiguous "war warning," nor did he direct him to dispense with some of the training activity and conduct the long-distance searches which might have detected the Japanese approach.

As Commander-in-Chief of the Pacific Fleet, Kimmel must bear the responsibility for his actions—or lack of them. That is one of the cold, hard maxims of the profession he chose to follow. But his rationale for not ordering a massive search effort may not have been entirely faulty. Altogether, Bellinger had only eighty-one patrol planes. Twenty-seven of these were worn from hard training use. Fifty-four were new types, for which there were not enough spare parts for a sustained long-distance reconnaissance operation. These planes and their crews were already heavily taxed by the tempo of the stepped-up training routine. Kimmel knew that when war came they would be sorely needed for deployment at advanced bases, in support of U.S. counter-initiatives launched against the enemy. Meanwhile, it did not seem prudent to exhaust these valuable but overworked assets by boring holes in the sky. So it was that December 7, 1941, only seven Catalinas were aloft, three on a morning security patrol and four conducting training activities. At the same time the enemy striking force had begun to launch its planes from a position only 230 miles north of Oahu, just as Bellinger and Martin had predicted several months before.

Trying to salvage one of the PBYs which was caught at its moorings at Kaneohe Bay. Despite these efforts the plane was sunk in a subsequent strafing attack. (U.S. Navy)

The day dawned pleasant and sunny with a light ten-knot breeze from the north. Scattered cumulus clouds accented the clear blue sky and congregated over the mountains. The first indication that this day would somehow be different came from one of the Catalinas operating out of the new naval air station at Kaneohe Bay where Commander Knefler "Soc" McGinnis commanded Patrol Wing 1 with three squadrons of PBYs. At 0715, Ensign Bill Tanner, pilot of 14-P-1 radioed to base that he had attacked a submarine off the entrance to Pearl Harbor. This was one of the five two-man Japanese submarines whose mission it was to penetrate harbor defenses, providing last-minute intelligence information and later joining in the attack. But to those ashore, Tanner's report was nothing short of incredible and their first reaction was that a U.S. submarine had wandered into the defensive area and had come under attack by mistake. While this possibility was being checked out, Japanese dive bombers arrived over Ford Island and began their attack. The first plane screamed out of the sky at 0755 to place its bomb on the parking apron

11

near VP-22's hangar. Pat Bellinger's operations officer, Commander Logan Ramsey, did two things almost simultaneously. He directed his radioman to broadcast an electrifying message to the world. "AIR RAID PEARL HARBOR—THIS IS NO DRILL."[7] While this message was going out, he picked up the phone and notified his boss what was occurring.

On that fateful morning Pat Bellinger was in his quarters at the opposite end of Ford Island, recuperating from a debilitating case of the flu. His jaw tightened as he listened intently to Ramsey's hurried report. "I'll be right down," he said, and began pulling on his clothes.[8] Suddenly the house was rocked by an earth-shaking blast as Japanese pilots found their mark on the *Arizona* which was moored not far from the housing area. Bellinger quickly herded his family into the basement, which had once been an ammunition storage bunker. In the hours that followed, it would become an air-raid shelter for other families and a first-aid station for wounded personnel. Then he jumped into his car with Lieutenant Commander Charlie Coe, an officer from his staff, and made a wild dash for his headquarters.

It was not a long ride, perhaps no more than a mile, but that day it seemed much further. Bellinger drove fast amid explosions and flying debris. The road ran close to the water and the two officers were provided with a panoramic view of the incredible disaster that was unfolding around them. It was an experience Pat Bellinger would never forget. "Dreadful things were happening to ships berthed alongside Ford Island . . ." he later recalled. "They were being torpedoed and bombed and some were sinking." Men from those ships were swimming in the water and some had begun to come ashore "covered with oil and with their clothes partly blown off."[9] Several were badly burned.

Although it seemed an interminable period of time since Logan Ramsey had alerted him, Bellinger arrived at operations while the first attack was still in progress. Despite the destruction all around him he was determined to get additional PBY aircraft aloft to search out the Japanese carriers which were out there somewhere waiting to retrieve their brood. To his dismay, the Japanese had done their job well. There was only one Catalina on Ford Island which was still flyable and he could not launch it because it was hemmed in by burning aircraft and rubble. To make things worse, the radio link with Kaneohe Bay was not functioning and he could not immediately determine what assets Soc McGinnis might be able to muster.

As it turned out, the situation there was no better. In fact the Japanese planes had hit Kaneohe Bay about five minutes before the first attack on Ford Island. Nine fighters had come in low, machine-gunning the control tower and four pitifully helpless PBYs moored in the bay. Then they

A PATWING 2 seaplane hangar is gutted. (U.S. Navy)

Many PBYs were destroyed in the Pearl Harbor conflagration (U.S. Navy)

13

circled and commenced another low-level strafing run, this time concentrating their efforts on the planes on the parking apron.

There can be no mistake about it: the Japanese onslaught had caught the Americans completely by surprise. But it was only a matter of minutes before PBY crewmen and ground personnel shook off their astonishment and managed to get a few machine guns into action against the enemy. Others centered their attention on saving those planes not completely engulfed in flame and on moving salvageable aircraft away from those which were beyond recovery. They were aided in their efforts by a brief lull in the attack. But before they could make much progress enemy fighters struck again.

At about 0930 a formation of nine two-place bombers came in over Kaneohe Bay at about a thousand feet. They scored a hit on one of the seaplane hangars, killing a number of men who were inside handling ammunition. A second wave of bombing planes followed close on the heels of the first but did little additional damage. Then at about 1000 there was a final strafing attack. By this time a number of machine guns had been set up on makeshift mounts and these downed two of the Japanese fighters.

The planes which had been on patrol, and those which had taken off from Ford Island that morning to practice tactics with a U.S. submarine, were at first unaware of the Japanese attack. Lieutenant (j.g.) Charlie Hibberd of VP-24 was operating off the island of Maui and had just made radio contact with the exercise submarine. He and his crew considered this a rare opportunity to sharpen their skills. But before they could begin the operation they received new instructions from the squadron commanding officer, Commander John Fitzsimmons, who was also airborne that morning for antisubmarine practice. They were directed to break off the exercise immediately and to conduct a patrol in accordance with prearranged air-raid plans. Hibberd remembers that:

> The skipper also ordered us to man our machine guns which I thought was being a little eager. I was cursing the fact that they would call an air-raid drill just when we, for the first time, were going to have a chance to practice with a submarine. Vaguely I can recall looking ahead as we approached Oahu and seeing smoke in the distance but it seemed quiet as we flew west on the first leg of the patrol. At about that time I heard another pilot yell over the air-raid frequency that he was being attacked. I became alarmed at the tone of his voice. It sounded very authentic. Anyhow, I got on the mike and called the skipper to ask if this was an air-raid drill . . . or what. In a few moments he came back with, "Anyone who

14

thinks this is a drill had better forget it." About that time my radioman came up to the cockpit with a message typed in red which said, 'The Japanese have made an attack on Pearl Harbor.' "[10]

Meanwhile, Pat Bellinger grimly continued his efforts to get more planes in the air. The enemy fleet had to be located. By this time, however, it was far from clear what might be done, even if the Japanese striking force was found. It was a frustrating experience.

After the first attack on Ford Island, Bellinger was finally able to reestablish contact with Kaneohe Bay to learn that only two PBYs at that facility were still flyable. He ordered them into the air immediately and then all communications were again lost. When the link was finally restored, Kaneohe reported that the two flyable aircraft had also been put out of commission.

On Ford Island, Lieutenant Commander Massie Hughes, Commanding Officer of VP-25, was somehow able to skirt the burning rubble with the wing's last flyable PBY, and get airborne. This was accomplished while the second attack on Ford Island was in full swing and as he lifted off he found himself enveloped in a hail of friendly but indiscriminate antiaircraft fire. Miraculously, the plane kept on flying and he quickly cleared the area.

By about 1000 the Japanese aircraft had completed their mission and were heading back to their floating bases in triumph. Some had already arrived. Commander Mitsuo Fuchida, who had led the first wave, made a glowing report to the fleet commander and recommended a second attack. But Vice Admiral Chuichi Nagumo was a cautious man. He had achieved a victory beyond his fondest expectations and he did not intend to press his luck. A course to the northwest was ordered and the fleet retired.

In the meantime, Charlie Hibberd had flown out on his assigned track until his calculations told him that he had just enough fuel to return to base. He had taken off that morning with considerably less than a full fuel load because he expected to be gone only long enough to conduct exercises with a U.S. submarine. Hibberd knew that while he had been out on his search the base had been under heavy Japanese air attack, but he was not entirely prepared for what he found upon landing. He touched down in the lower channel, just off the stern of the stricken battleship *Nevada*. She had gotten underway, but was torpedoed, dive-bombed, and then deliberately run aground to prevent her being sunk in the main channel to the sea. As Hibberd taxied to his buoy there was fire and smoke and frantic activity everywhere. When they pulled him up the ramp he was appalled at the sight which greeted him. "What a mess," he

15

Stunned officials and military planners had to assess the damage and determine what was left to fight with. (U.S. Navy)

recalls. "I couldn't believe my eyes. Many of the PBYs were destroyed as was one of the main hangars."[11]

The fires at Ford Island and Kaneohe Bay were slowly brought under control, but in Pearl Harbor itself oil from the sunken and twisted ships floated on the water's surface and continued to burn into the night. The attack on the great naval base was over, but the war in the Pacific had just begun. Pat Bellinger and his squadron commanding officers now faced the task of assessing damage and determining what was left to fight with. The latter was a prime consideration at this point, for nobody knew when the Japanese might return.

At Kaneohe Bay, twenty-six Catalinas had been completely destroyed and seven others badly damaged. The three aircraft which remained flyable were those which had been in the air at the time of the attack, and one of these had been riddled with holes by the Japanese fighters. At Ford Island, the picture was not much brighter. Late in the day ground crews had succeeded in getting four PBYs into flying condition. These were launched as soon as they achieved "up" status and were dispatched to look for the Japanese fleet, which by then was steaming away. Those Catalinas beyond repair were cannibalized for parts and consigned to the junk heap. Others deemed salvageable were painstakingly put back into service. By the following day enough aircraft were resurrected to begin long-distance patrols. It was a case of closing the barn door after the horse had been stolen.

The problem now as Bellinger saw it was to strike back—but how? The fast carriers *Enterprise* and *Lexington* which had been at sea on December 7 and others like the *Saratoga* and *Yorktown* would be at the heart of the new American striking force. But what of the PBYs? He had watched the sleek Japanese fighters as they made their low-level attacks on Ford Island. They were fast and highly maneuverable, and could climb like nothing he had ever seen. The men that flew them were good—very good, and hardly the myopic orientals that Americans had always imagined them to be. How could the docile old PBYs survive in the air against an enemy like that? Although no one had yet made the point, he knew that many of his pilots and flight-crew members had seen what he had seen and were asking themselves the same question. Perhaps it was just as well that he had not had more aircraft in the air that morning. It might have been even worse.

What he needed now was a new type of patrol bomber. Something faster, more heavily armed, able to fight back against marauding fighters and, more important, able to carry the fight to the enemy wherever he might be found. But he knew that no such aircraft were yet available. What he would get if he was lucky was more PBYs because they were the only patrol aircraft then being produced in quantity. Somehow, they would have to learn how to use the PBYs effectively.

2

The Desperate Days

In the Philippine Islands, a few thousand miles to the west, the Japanese assault had not been unexpected. Admiral Thomas C. Hart who commanded the U.S. Asiatic Fleet was awakened in the early hours of December 8 and informed of the Japanese attack on Pearl Harbor. In Hawaii it was still the 7th.

Hart had long believed that war between the United States and Japan was simply a matter of the latter country choosing the most propitious time to strike. And when that time came, he knew that the Philippines would be a priority target for Japanese invasion. In anticipation of that eventuality he had ordered all Navy dependents out of the islands almost a year before. This had not endeared him to many wives nor to some of his personnel, who considered the action overcautious and premature.

But Hart knew that when war erupted, the United States would be hard-pressed to hold these islands. The Asiatic Fleet was not an impressive force compared to the enormous assets of the Japanese in this part of the world. Hart's force consisted of one heavy cruiser, two light cruisers, thirteen old destroyers, a couple of old gunboats and a number of minesweepers, tenders, and auxiliary vessels. He also had a respectable submarine force and two squadrons of PBY-4 Catalina flying boats which made up Patrol Wing 10, under Captain Frank D. Wagner.

The pilots and crews of Patrol Squadrons 101 and 102, commanded by Lieutenant Commander John V. Peterson and Lieutenant Commander Edgar T. Neale respectively, had known for several days that something was about to happen in the western Pacific. During the last weeks of

18

November and into December they had scoured the South China Sea for signs of an impending Japanese strike and had found nothing. Then on December 2 they came upon a concentration of Japanese merchant ships, including transports, which had begun to congregate in Camranh Bay on the coast of what was then French Indochina. On the following day this force had grown to fifty ships, with cruisers and destroyers now plainly in evidence. But by the 4th the entire armada had slipped away and headed south under cover of bad weather. The Americans did not know where the Japanese were headed but they knew that a force of that size and composition was up to no good. It was not seen again until located by the British a few days later in the Gulf of Siam. Meanwhile, PBYs searching the northeast sector of the South China Sea had begun to encounter Japanese reconnaissance aircraft off the coast of Luzon. There were tense moments as planes from each side passed within sight of one another, guns at the ready.

Whatever was brewing, Frank Wagner was taking no chances. He was acutely aware that his twenty-eight Catalinas and a few float planes made up the sum total of naval air forces in that part of the world and he did not want them wiped out by a sudden and unexpected Japanese thrust. Consequently, by the time the shooting started, he had dispersed his aircraft to several different locations. Approximately one-fourth of the PBYs were based at Sangley Point across from the Cavite Naval Base on Manila Bay. Another detachment operated from the town of Los Banos on the southernmost end of Laguna de Bay, a freshwater lake south of Manila, while seven more of the big patrol planes were assigned to Olongopo on Subic Bay. Still another contingent operated from the seaplane tender *Childs* anchored off the city of Manila itself, while far to the south on the island of Mindanao three PBYs patrolled the Davao Gulf and the easternmost approaches to the Celebes Sea, supported by the tender *William B. Preston*. On the western fringes, the *Heron* was positioned off the southern end of the island of Palawan. From this location she dispatched her small float planes to patrol the Balabac Strait, thus providing coverage of the western approaches to the Sulu and Celebes Seas. Further preparations were made by stocking a number of carefully chosen locations with aviation fuel and supplies to give the Catalinas maximum operating flexibility.

By the time the sun was up on December 8 all available PBYs of PATWING 10 had been dispersed for wartime operations. Chief Aviation Pilot Earl D. Payne remembered that they "were routed out in the dark at 4 o'clock in the morning to get their planes ready—motors warmed up, bombs, torpedoes, and depth charges loaded, food for the pilots and crew, and all other necessary preparations made."[1] Approximately half of the

19

available aircraft would be employed to seek out the enemy, while the other half would remain at their assigned locations in a ready status, to be launched as striking forces once the whereabouts of the enemy became known. Unfortunately, it was the enemy who would be first to find them.

At Malalag Bay in the Davao Gulf one of three aircraft from VP-101 assigned to the tender *William B. Preston* took off before dawn and proceeded south in search of the Japanese, according to plan. The remaining two Catalinas, 101-P-4 and 101-P-7, rode quietly at anchor in the early-morning light with full bomb loads, awaiting the order for an attack mission. Suddenly, without warning, enemy dive bombers arrived on the scene and commenced an immediate attack. The *Preston* somehow escaped damage and dispatched one of the attackers with her guns, but the PBYs were sitting ducks. The two hapless seaplanes were strafed and sunk in a matter of minutes. One of the pilots died in that attack.

But the *Preston* and her two planes were small potatoes. The main focus of Japanese attention in the early hours of the war in the Philippines were the Army Air Forces on Luzon to the north. Just hours after the destruction of the PBYs at Malalag Bay, the enemy launched à series of major air attacks on airfields in the Manila area and destroyed large numbers of aircraft on the ground. By the end of the third day of the war, the Japanese had effectively secured control of the skies over the Philippines. For the Catalinas of PATWING 10, this meant that henceforth they must stand virtually unprotected against the air might of Japan. That was the hand they were dealt and they had no choice but to play with it. Everyone knew that the game would be rough for the next few months but no one foresaw the grim reality of what lay ahead.

Early on the morning of December 10 Lieutenant Clarence A. Keller, Jr., who had been searching the northeast sector of the South China Sea, located a powerful enemy surface force about 250 miles west of Luzon. He reported his find to PATWING 10 and then set about shadowing the Japanese, using the clouds to cover himself.

This was the kind of opportunity Frank Wagner had been waiting for and he immediately dispatched Lieutenant Commander John Peterson with five PBYs of VP-101, each loaded with four 500-pound bombs. They flew northwest from their temporary base at Los Banos until about 1050 local time, when they began picking up MO signals from Keller who was still maintaining contact. The MO transmission was the standard procedure by which a radioman of one aircraft sent the letter M (two dashes) followed by the letter O (three dashes) in succession, providing a homing signal for other friendly aircraft.

Shortly thereafter Peterson's five planes altered course and headed

Admiral Thomas C. Hart, Commander Asiatic Fleet.
(U.S. Navy)

straight for Keller's signal, sighting the enemy ships visually about
1135. The Japanese were well aware that they had been discovered and
had launched two float planes earlier in an attempt to silence Keller or at
least drive him off. Somehow he had managed to elude them. Now as the
PBYs approached they could see the enemy formation through the clouds
below executing a classic high-speed zig-zag pattern in anticipation of an
attack. It was a force small in numbers but it packed plenty of muscle
consisting as it did of three large warships and two escorts.*

Peterson kept his planes in formation and executed a high-altitude
bombing run. Ensign Russell F. Chambers had been assigned the job of
master bomber and it was he who would be responsible for calling the
drop. Peterson maneuvered to ensure that his planes would have a clear
view of the target at drop time. He had singled out the largest of the
enemy warships which was steaming in the center of the disposition.

*Peterson's report of the action states that there were two battleships, one cruiser and
two destroyers. In fact, this was probably Admiral Takahashi's Third Fleet covering
force, consisting of two heavy cruisers, one light cruiser, and two destroyer types
converted to seaplane tenders.

About sixty seconds prior to release the Japanese opened up with a formidable barrage of antiaircraft fire. A half-minute later the Japanese began to get the range and the American plane crews had their first experience with ack-ack. Despite this they maintained formation well and twenty bombs were released on signal. Four of the PBYs then headed for cloud cover to escape the increasingly accurate antiaircraft fire. Peterson put his plane into a diving turn to make Japanese fire control more difficult, meanwhile observing the attack's results.

Most of the bombs had fallen in the water behind the target, but one exploded close astern and another appeared to be a direct hit on the fantail. As Peterson and his crew watched, the big ship began a 360-degree turn to port which took it out of the formation. Finally it settled on a heading of about 020 degrees, which it maintained at reduced speed. There was no evidence of fire aboard the Japanese warship but Peterson thought it likely that the steering system and perhaps the screws had been damaged.[2]

In all, he felt it had been a well-executed attack, but the extent of damage to the enemy was impossible to determine with accuracy. Only one of the PBYs had been hit by antiaircraft fire, and the damage was insignificant. The five planes joined up at about 3,000 feet and reported completion of the strike by radio to PATWING 10. Two of the strike planes were assigned to relieve Keller and his crew in attempting to maintain contact with the enemy. The PATWING 10 commander felt that with some luck a second attack might yet put the warship, which was thought to be wounded, out of action. In the meantime, Peterson and the remaining aircraft returned to Los Banos.

Back at Sangley Point four PBYs were hurriedly armed with torpedoes for the mission. As they circled on the water making their engine checks and preparing for take-off, Japanese planes converged on the Cavite Naval Base to deal it a crippling blow. The heavily loaded PBYs milling about near the target area were bonus points. As they struggled to get into the air the attack began, with Japanese escort fighters swarming over them. Lieutenant Harmon T. Utter in 101-P-5 and Ensign James H. McConnell in 102-P-28 managed to stagger into the air but their aircraft were so badly shot up that they were obliged to land a short distance from the base. Utter's gunners shot down one of the enemy attackers before Utter was forced to execute an emergency open-sea landing some twelve miles offshore. Both this aircraft and McConnell's were eventually able to taxi to shore for repairs. The two remaining PBYs in the four-plane flight fared somewhat better. They too got airborne and were able to shake the Japanese, who were more interested in the destruction of Cavite. But they could not locate the straggling warship or the rest of the

Japanese surface force. That night they returned to Sangley Point to find the nearby Cavite Naval Base in shambles. The extensive damage and the loss of the large radio antenna on the base resulted in a decision by Captain Wagner to move the PATWING 10 staff aboard the tender *Childs* to ensure continued communications with his PBYs.

Perhaps more serious than the destruction of the Cavite Naval Base were the amphibious landings that day by Japanese invasion forces at Aparri and Vigan in the northern half of Luzon. That meant that enemy troops were now ashore in significant numbers and could soon be expected to move south toward Manila and the U.S. bases. But additional landings might still be prevented, thus slowing the Japanese juggernaut and buying precious time for the defenders.

With this goal in mind, the seven PBYs based at Olongopo took off on the 12th to hunt for a large Japanese invasion force which was believed moving down the west coast of Luzon. They searched the area with a fine-toothed comb but turned up no trace of the enemy. When their fuel was exhausted they returned to base, taxied to their buoys, and cut the engines. After some rest they would try again. It was at precisely this point that they were attacked by Japanese fighters.

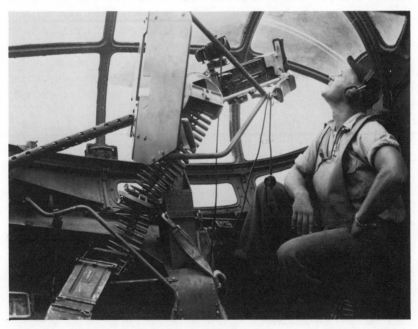

Scanning the sky for enemy planes. (U.S. Navy)

It is entirely conceivable that the PBYs were followed home and pounced upon when they were most vulnerable. But the confident Japanese had shown no predisposition to avoid aerial combat. The fact is that the sky for many miles around Manila now belonged to the enemy and it is probable that the PBYs were merely targets of opportunity. In any event, the fighters made short work of the helpless waterbirds, destroying all seven at their moorings.

Now there were only seventeen of the original twenty-eight planes remaining. Of these, no more than eleven were in flying condition. The other six were in varying states of disrepair. Olongopo itself came in for a drubbing on the 14th, the Japanese planes making rubble of buildings, roads, and bridges. The Cavite Naval Base had already been rendered practically useless on the 10th and it was only a matter of time before General MacArthur would be forced to declare Manila an open city. Frank Wagner later observed: "We had entered into a war with an enemy who, quite frankly, was much smarter than we expected him to be. He had airplanes that performed better than we had expected; he used them in numbers and in concentrations against proper objectives in a manner that exceeded our estimates of his ability."[3] The Japanese were good, there was no doubt about it. In less than a week the situation for Admiral Hart's forces had become untenable. Faced with a difficult decision, he reluctantly ordered them to move south to prevent their destruction.

On the morning of the 15th the PBYs which were still flyable took off for Lake Lanao on Mindanao, where they would have a short stopover on their way south. Their destination was the Dutch East Indies. Six planes remained in the Manila area and it was hoped that three, possibly four, of these might be restored to flying condition so that they could eventually join the others.

The *Childs*, with Captain Wagner and the PATWING 10 staff aboard, also headed south to link up again with the PBYs and the tenders *Heron* and *William B. Preston* at Surabaja on Java a few days before Christmas. The evolution was accomplished with little enemy opposition, although the *Childs* was attacked by a Japanese flying boat at Manado on Celebes Island, and PBY number 24 of VP-102 was sunk on Lake Lanao when it struck a rock. The number of available Catalinas had now been reduced to ten, and on December 23 these aircraft were combined into one squadron under Lieutenant Commander John Peterson. Lieutenant Keller took four of these planes and set up operations at the Dutch base at Ambon, over a thousand miles to the east in the Banda Sea. Most of the others followed a few days later.

Back in the Philippines four of the six planes which were left behind had been put back into service. But by this time the situation had become so precarious that they were obliged to remain heavily camouflaged and carefully hidden during daylight hours, venturing forth only after dark. On Christmas Eve, Lieutenant Harmon Utter and his crew left their hiding place on the shore of Laguna de Bay and flew the short distance to Cavite. There they picked up a large number of passengers, including the Commander of Army Air Forces in the Philippines, Major General Lewis H. Brereton, and his staff, who were to be evacuated to the Dutch East Indies. Of necessity, no lights were used and the big seaplane pushed off into a black night and taxied cautiously out to open water for the take-off run. Utter eased the throttles to full power and the heavily laden aircraft moved forward laboriously and heaved itself up and onto the step. At that moment a motor launch making the run from Manila to Cavite, and also running without lights, loomed ahead of the speeding Catalina. Utter was too close to lift off and clear the launch. He chopped the power and stood on the right rudder. The plane careened to starboard, avoiding the boat but badly damaging one of the wing floats.

General Brereton and the other evacuees were flown out in another aircraft but Utter's plane was again temporarily out of commission. Worse, it was necessary to beach the aircraft in the open where it was clearly visible from the air. The coming of daylight would mean almost certain destruction by marauding Japanese planes. All during the night the crew worked by the light of flashlights shielding the beams as best they could with their hands. As the sun poked its head over the horizon, men threw their tools aboard and the engines were started. The fix held and the plane returned to Laguna de Bay where it was beached alongside another PBY and quickly camouflaged to blend with the jungle foliage.

No sooner had this been accomplished when Japanese reconnaissance aircraft arrived on the scene, photographing the area and searching for signs of any American planes which might be hiding there. They apparently spotted the PBYs because around noon that same day (which also happened to be Christmas), twin-engine bombers appeared and commenced a savage bombing and strafing attack on the spot where the PBYs were hidden. The attack completely destroyed Utter's aircraft and sank the plane alongside. A third aircraft in the same general vicinity was also lost to the enemy assault.

These were black days for the U.S. forces, devoted to survival and a few desperate attempts to strike back. In the meantime, the well-oiled Japanese war machine spread southward, establishing bases from which to consolidate ill-gotten gains—bases from which to sally forth again on its mission of conquest. One of these was located at Jolo on an island of the same name about 150 miles northeast of Borneo, between the Sulu and Celebes Seas. Meanwhile, at Ambon, more than 800 miles to the south,

Frank Wagner's PBYs and their crews, bloody but unbowed, were preparing a raid on Jolo to let the Japanese know that they could not rest securely.

Sometime before midnight on December 26, six PBY-4 Catalinas began taking off one by one to join up in two sections overhead. Each was loaded with three 500-pound bombs and enough fuel for approximately sixteen hours in the air. The idea was to catch an over-confident enemy with a dawn surprise at his anchorage, hit hard, and run. It would turn out to be a hair-raising experience for all those involved. For Lieutenant Burden R. Hastings, pilot of 101-P-1 and leader of the strike, it would be his last flight. He and his crew would not return.

The six planes headed northwest and crew members settled in their individual niches for the long flight. There were the usual trips back and forth to the coffee pot and some scattered conversation, but mostly there was just the endless wait as they moved slowly across the night sky. The engines had been leaned out to save fuel and this resulted in reduced airspeeds. Hastings' plane was especially slow, which made for a somewhat ragged formation as the others struggled to keep station.

At about 0200 in the morning, the second section, led by Lieutenant John J. Hyland, lost contact with the three aircraft of section one and proceeded independently to the target. These planes made the remainder of the trip at a slightly faster speed and came upon the island of Jolo at the crack of dawn. Section one was nowhere in sight and Hyland felt that it was still not light enough for an effective bombing run, so he turned the formation eastward to await dawn.[4]

Hyland's plane was not equipped with a bombsight and the lead was turned over to Lieutenant (j.g.) T. E. L. McCabe in 101-P-23, one of whose pilots would function as master bomber. Tom McCabe began his run in toward the island at about 0625 at which time he judged there was just enough light in the sky to do the job.[5]

The enemy had probably been alerted by the earlier approach to the island, for now the ships anchored off the town, three cruisers and two transports, put up a fierce barrage of antiaircraft fire. The bomber in 23 boat did not like the way the approach was developing and called for a turn to gain altitude and get into a better position. As they made the turn, they were engaged by eight enemy fighters which came in fast with guns blazing. The three Catalinas made for cloud cover. 101-P-11 was so badly worked over that she could no longer remain airborne and her pilot, Ensign Leroy C. Deede, set her down in the open sea. Meanwhile Hastings arrived at Jolo with section one and began an immediate attack. By then, the hornets' nest had been aroused. The air was alive with enemy fighters and the antiaircraft fire was very heavy.

26

Looking forward from the starboard blister of a PBY. (U.S. Navy)

Ensign E. L. Christman flying 101-P-9 became aware that he was under fighter attack when he heard the chattering of his own waist guns. One of the enemy planes which had gotten too close to these guns was hit. It rolled over on its back and fell off into a fatal spin. The others dropped their belly tanks and came in for another pass. At about this time the PBYs broke formation, and each plane concentrated on making its own drop. Hastings' 101-P-1 was last seen diving toward the enemy ships. He and his crew were never heard from again.

Christman released his bombs on one of the cruisers with a 60-degree dive angle, at two hundred knots indicated air speed. He pulled out at 5,000 feet and headed west. One of the fighters stayed with him, making repeated attacks from the port quarter. Christman countered by turning into the oncoming aircraft, and by this method was able to throw off the pilot's aim on several runs. This went on for some twenty minutes until the fighter's 20-mm cannon found its mark and holed one of the PBY's fuel tanks. High-octane avgas began to pour into the plane through the

27

mechanic's compartment in the pylon supporting the big parasol wing. On the next pass another 20-mm projectile exploded inside the fuselage near the radio operator's position, and the aircraft burst into flames.

Although 101-P-9 was now at an altitude of 1,000 feet, the second radioman and the second mechanic elected to jump and got clear of the aircraft at about 300 feet. Both made it safely into the water. The first mechanic had been killed by one of the fighter's hits. Christman, in the meantime, fought the controls of the burning plane and managed an open-sea landing. Then he and the remaining three crew members abandoned the stricken aircraft which sank a few minutes later.

R. L. Pettit, the first radioman, was badly burned and had to be assisted in the water. It was decided that the copilot, Ensign William Gough, a strong swimmer, would try to make it to shore and get help from the natives. Christman and the third pilot Chief D. D. Lurvey stayed with Pettit and the three slowly made for an island perhaps twenty miles distant. Pettit did not survive the swim but Christman and Lurvey swam through the night, and after twenty-nine hours were plucked out of the water by natives.

Ensign Gough was also picked up that day in a state of exhaustion by Moro boatmen and taken to a small village where he was cared for by a Philippine schoolteacher. His pleas for a search party to look for the others went unheeded. Later he was taken to another island where he was reunited with the second radioman who had parachuted from the burning aircraft. There he learned that the second mechanic, who had also jumped, had died of his wounds during the long swim.[6]

Ensign Jack Dawley in 101-P-6, the other aircraft in Hasting's three-plane section, had no better time of it than Christman. As he began his bombing run his PBY was hit by antiaircraft fire from the ships but she was still flying, so he kept on toward the target. Then the fighters hit them and both Dawley's waist gunners were killed. The first mechanic Evren C. McLawhorn manned both guns, switching from one side to the other as the fighters came in. He was hit seven times in both arms and legs, took a sliver of shrapnel in one eye, but kept on shooting anyhow. The fire was now intense and it was clear to Dawley that he would never complete the planned horizontal bombing run. He pushed the nose over and dove for one of the cruisers, releasing his three 500-pounders by seaman's eye. Then he pulled up and tried to shake the fighters. It was a valiant attempt, but before long the enemy planes had punctured the fuel tanks and cut the rudder-control cables. The starboard engine had been hit by cannon fire or an antiaircraft burst, and was wheezing its last. Dawley still had aileron and elevator control and he used these, plus the remaining power from the good port engine, to jockey the big plane down

28

and onto the water a few hundred yards from the beach and a small native village. As the plane touched down it burst into flames. The surviving crew members jumped into the water and attempted to put some distance between themselves and the burning aircraft. One of the enemy fighters came down to strafe the plane before it sank.

Dawley and the others swam toward shore and were soon met by natives in dugout canoes. They carried spears and bolo knives and there was some question as to whether or not the American would be well received. A shouted "Hello Joe" from one of the crewmen, however, brought a friendly response. They were picked up and brought to shore where they were given first-aid treatment and taken into the village.

Dawley and the other survivors from his aircraft were soon reunited with Christman and his crew, with the help of the locals. Together, with further native assistance, they proceeded along the Sulu Archipelago to Tawau on North Borneo and then south to Tarakan. From there they continued via Dutch Dornier flying boat to Balikpapen. At this point Dawley and the wounded but indestructible McLawhorn boarded a commercial airliner for Surabaja. At 1230 on January 10, 1942, Dawley walked into headquarters, U.S. Naval Forces and filed his report. Christman and the others arrived two days later by steamer.[7]

Of the six PBYs that had left Ambon on December 26, only two had returned to base. Leroy Deede and the entire crew of 101-P-11 were rescued by a PATWING 10 Catalina on the 28th. Word-of-mouth reports from natives who had witnessed the attack on Jolo indicated that some

The Cavite naval base had been rendered practically useless by enemy bombers.

damage had been inflicted on the enemy and that possibly one transport had been sunk. Unfortunately, the accuracy of such reports could not be confirmed.

Dawley, in assessing the Jolo mission, stated flatly the opinion of himself and others. "PBY aircraft," he said, "are too slow for successful bombing attacks against objectives which have good antiaircraft protection."[8] Christman was even more emphatic. "Under no circumstances," he said, "should PBY aircraft be used where they will come in contact with enemy fighter planes unless protected by fighter convoy."[9]

Their wisdom was sound but their recommendations were to no avail. There were no fighters available for escort missions, and no fast bombers to take the place of the PBYs.

3

Cold Turkey Alley

On the first day of January 1942 Admiral Hart arrived at Surabaja by submarine to regroup the units of the Asiatic Fleet which had already preceded him south. Other efforts of a multinational nature were already underway to bring available forces together for coordinated action against the common enemy. By January 15 a combined organization called American, British, Dutch and Australian Command (ABDACOM) was formed under British Field Marshall Sir Archibald Wavell. The idea was theoretically sound, but in practical application it fell far short of expectations. The Japanese had moved rapidly down the Malay peninsula to the Malacca Strait by the middle of December, and the British were adamant in their insistence that Singapore be defended at all costs. The Dutch were sympathetic to the British position but were understandably much more concerned for the safety of Sumatra and Java, while the Australians viewed with growing alarm the very real possibility that the enemy would drive through the Malay barrier and threaten Australia itself. Each national force was preoccupied with its own geographical area of concern. The Americans, who had no proprietary interest in this part of the world, concentrated their efforts on the eastern flank of the ABDA Command, an area which extended roughly from the east coast of Borneo to the western end of New Guinea and northward into the Celebes Sea. To the pilots and crews of PATWING 10 with their tired and battle-scarred Catalinas, this sector became known, in the grim humor that always accompanies war, as "Cold Turkey Alley."

The hard-pressed wing got some reinforcement in January when it was bolstered by the arrival of twelve PBYs from Patrol Squadron 22. These were immediately thrown into the fray, and there was plenty for them to do. The Japanese continued their methodical advance southward, securing operating bases for their ships, and airfields from which they could provide land-based air cover for each step along the way. It continued to be an unhealthy environment for Catalinas.

January 11 brought yet another success story for the Japanese. On that day they drove south again, making successful landings on Tarakan Island, strategically located at the northern end of the Makassar Strait, and on the Manado Peninsula of Celebes, giving them a commanding position on the Molucca Sea. Seven Army Air Force B-17s from Malang Field on Java went after the invasion force at Tarakan. Four of them failed to reach their destination due to bad weather, and the three that found the target dropped their bombs from almost 30,000 feet through an undercast—and, as may be expected, scored no hits.

Four PBYs from PATWING 10 did little better. They took off at about 0300 from their base at Ambon and flew north to oppose the landing at Manado. Other long-range ABDA aircraft also made attacks on the invasion force. But in all it was a pitiful response to an important enemy operation supported by two aircraft carriers and three heavy cruisers. The PBYs were engaged by Type 97 floatplane fighters, just south of Manado. Ensign Jack L. Grayson in 101-P-7 saw them coming and ducked into the clouds for cover. It was at that inopportune moment that his tired and overworked port engine simply stopped running and he was left hanging in the air on one good engine, with a full load of bombs and several Japanese fighters on his tail. As he broke clear of the clouds he jettisoned his bombs to lighten the load and observed that he now had only two fighters to contend with. That was enough to make survival very tenuous. After a few runs on the crippled PBY the enemy seaplanes had completely disabled the good engine. Grayson nosed the big Cat over and dove for the water to make an open-sea, dead-stick landing. He set her down lightly about sixty miles southeast of Manado. Then he and his crew quickly abandoned the aircraft and swam away as the two fighters made strafing runs in an attempt to sink her. Although they made numerous hits, the tough old Cat refused to go under and the fighters soon gave up and left the area. Seeing this, the crew swam back to the aircraft and attempted to get out a radio message for help. It was no use. The plane was now settling low in the water and it was time for a final departure. Jettisoning the bombsight and all classified materials, they inflated the large rubber life raft and piled into it with all the C rations and other food they could find, plus about ten gallons of water. Their departure was timely because when they had gotten no more than five

Waist gunner and his .50-caliber mount. (U.S. Navy)

hundred yards away the mortally wounded old Cat sank out of sight.

They were alone on a hostile sea where the enemy roamed at will virtually unopposed. They were concerned that enemy aircraft might find them before they got to shore, so to avoid detection they camouflaged the rubber raft with blue dungarees.

All the first day and through the night they paddled without raising land. It soon became clear that they were wasting their strength with little to show for it. A sail was rigged in an attempt to take advantage of the wind but mostly they just bobbed about in the blistering sun. In the early-morning hours of the 16th they encountered a new worry, in the form of a violent storm with twenty-foot waves that threatened to upend the raft. By first light, however, the storm had subsided, and they found that the high winds which had almost drowned them a few hours before had also driven them within sight of land. Despite their weakened condition they began paddling again in earnest, using the last of their energy. They feared that if they did not take this opportunity, they would drift by the island and into the open sea again. All through that day and night they worked closer, sometimes not certain whether they were making any headway at all in the blunt unwieldy raft. But by 1400 the following day they came ashore on the island of Mangole. There they discovered that exhaustion and exposure to the tropic sun had rendered most of them too weak to stand for more than a few minutes at a time.

Grayson decided that they would rest under the trees the rest of that day and night to regain their strength. The next morning they struck out for a village on the other side of the island where they hoped to find friendly natives who would take them to nearby Sanana Island. Since Mangole was mountainous and three of the crewmen had lost their shoes while struggling in the water, they fashioned footwear by cutting up their life vests and lashing the material to their feet. The distance to be traveled was only about ten miles but it was rugged country and they moved slowly and painfully. Twelve hours later they reached the village on the southern shore. There they were well received by the local population who gave them food and provided a place to sleep for the night. The following day a native boat took them to Sanana where a Dutch official was able to get a radio message back to base informing PATWING 10 headquarters that Grayson and his crew were alive and well. On the 20th one of the newly arrived planes from VP-22 landed off Sanana and picked up the entire crew.[1]

On the morning that Grayson and company were bobbing about in their rubber raft trying to reach Mangole, Ensign J. F. Davis was looking for signs of enemy activity in the Gulf of Tomini to the north and west of the struggling castaways. He found what he was looking for when he was suddenly attacked by a single Japanese Zero which came at him from the port quarter. Davis turned sharply toward the fighter, disrupting the enemy pilot's aim and causing him to veer to the right to avoid a collision. On the second try the Zero dove on the Catalina from slightly above on the starboard side, with the PBY's waist gunner pumping out slugs as fast as his gun would fire. The fighter turned to the right as he passed under the big plane and reappeared off the nose in a wingover. It was a fatal mistake of an overconfident enemy. Davis, seeing his opportunity, slipped to the right, bringing, the port waist gunner into position to fire. One well-placed burst was all it took. The Zero burst into flames and plunged into the sea. The PBY crew suffered no injuries and although the plane took several hits, the actual damage was minimal.[2]

Davis' triumph was a tribute to superior pilot technique, excellent shooting by the waist gunner, and a bit of luck. Perhaps skill and aggressiveness could help even up the odds, at least when dealing with the enemy on a one-on-one basis. Unfortunately, this sort of success was the exception rather than the rule. In any case, there was no time or inclination for celebration. The Japanese war machine continued its victorious march southward. On January 23, invasion forces supported by Admiral Nagumo's powerful carrier striking force made a flanking movement and struck at Rabaul on the island of New Britain. There they easily overpowered the outnumbered Australian defenders and established a stronghold which they would retain until the end of the war. Now the enemy was in easy striking distance of New Guinea and the Solomons. There was justifiable American concern that he would soon spread south throughout the islands, denying Allied forces an island foothold from which to retake the area in the future, and cutting Australia off from the United States. The Japanese planners knew exactly what they were about.

Meanwhile, the Dutch base at Ambon had begun to come under heavy air attacks. Lieutenant D. G. "Ducky" Donaho arrived there on January 15 with two PBY reinforcements from VP-22.

We arrived at Ambon, perhaps midafternoon and in coming in for landings we were attacked by several Japanese Zeros. The starboard wing on 22-P-7 [Donaho's plane] was on fire very shortly and the plane was beached as soon as possible. No one was injured and only the starboard wing was damaged. 22-P-8 was not so fortunate. It was beached across the harbor from where we were and fire completely demolished it. One individual was injured by gunfire. All seaplanes and crews were evacuated the next day to Surabaja.[3]

Aircraft were a valuable commodity to the Allied forces, so Donaho and a repair crew returned a few days later and attempted to bring out the PBY they had beached. They worked through the night to fashion a temporary fix by covering the damaged wing with fabric.

Early next morning 22-P-7 and the repair aircraft took off for the return to Surabaja. Shortly after becoming airborne, the fabric on the damaged wing ballooned. We landed and taxied back to the mooring buoy, transferred personnel and equipment to the repair aircraft and returned to Surabaja.[4]

The situation at Ambon soon became untenable. By the 24th Japanese forces had occupied Kendari, only 350 miles away, and on that day carrier aircraft began a series of bombing raids to soften up the Dutch installation in preparation for invasion.

The fall of Ambon was now inevitable, and as the Japanese closed in for the kill, the PBYs kept the ABDA command advised of developments. Six Catalinas, under the command of Ducky Donaho, began operating from the tender *Heron* anchored in the Kai islands on February 1 and tracked the advance of the approaching enemy. One of these planes, 22-P-6, flown by Lieutenant Richard S. Bull, reconnoitered the Ambon area and radioed that it was under attack by Japanese fighters. Minutes later, although heavily engaged, Bull got out a second message in plain language which told the story. A large enemy force, including carriers, was

35

now at Ambon. Then the radio was silent. "There was no doubt in our minds what had happened to Bull, his aircraft and crew but there was no verification of the event until Ensign Hargraves [Bull's copilot] miraculously returned to Australia some time later. The aircraft had been shot down near Ambon and so far as I know he was the only one to survive."[5]

By February 4 all organized resistance by Dutch and Australian forces at Ambon had ceased. Some eight hundred miles to the west the situation was much the same. The PBYs had tracked an invasion force south through the Makassar Strait to the Dutch oil port of Balikpapen. Dutch aircraft had attacked with courage and skill but to no avail. On the night of January 24, four old U.S. four-stacker destroyers engaged the enemy and sank four transports and one patrol craft. But the enemy landing continued without further interruption.

The PBYs which had moved their base of operations to Surabaja found that it was no safe haven. On the day that Ambon fell, Japanese bombers and fighters set fire to several Dutch seaplanes and damaged a U.S. Navy Catalina on the water. That same afternoon Lieutenant (j.g.) Leroy Deede was attacked in the air by a Zero and shot it down. Another PBY was jumped by five Zeros over the Makassar Strait and managed to escape into the clouds.

The next day was much worse. The Japanese blasted Surabaja for an hour, starting at 1000. One Catalina was strafed and burned at its mooring. Another was caught inside a burning hangar and two 500-pound bombs detonated from the intense heat, destroying the plane and everything within a large radius. The officers' living quarters were completely demolished. In the afternoon 101-P-45, one of the PBY aircraft that had recently been turned over to the Americans by the Dutch, was shot down and presumed lost. By February 11, only twelve were left of a total of forty-five PATWING 10 aircraft.* Six of these were at Surabaja and six were at Darwin on the northern coast of Australia. Of the twelve remaining aircraft, only five were flyable and these had critically high engine times. It looked very much like the game was over for PATWING 10 and the Catalina flying boat in this part of the Pacific. But somehow they kept going. There simply was no other alternative. In fact the situation could get worse—and it did.

On February 16 the beleaguered British bastion at Singapore surrendered. This major victory had symbolic as well as strategic significance, but the Japanese did not stop to rest on their laurels. Palembang, the oil

*Total PATWING 10 aircraft refers to twenty-eight original PBYs of VP-101 and 102, reinforcements of twelve additional PBYs of VP-22, and five PBYs turned over to the Americans by the Dutch.

and trade center of Sumatra, and Bandjarmasin on the southeastern corner of Borneo, were successfully invaded that same day.* The seaport city of Makassar on the southwestern tip of Celebes Island had already been taken, and the enemy now set his sights on Java. His planes had been pounding the key Dutch naval base at Surabaja since February 3 and it was now time to tighten the vice. On the 18th an invasion force landed on the southeastern coast of Bali and quickly took possession of the nearby airfield. Now land-based air power could be brought to bear on Surabaja from a striking distance of about 150 miles. It had already become clear that Darwin, Australia, once considered as a fallback position for Allied naval forces, would not be suitable for that purpose because of its vulnerability to enemy attack. The spectacular and repeated successes of the Japanese had made them seem virtually invincible—and, for the moment, so they were.

At dawn on the 19th a powerful enemy strike force including both battleships and aircraft carriers arrived in the south Timor Sea and

*A February 14 paratroop attack on Palembang had been repulsed, but on the 16th of that month the enemy invaded in force.

The Japanese attack on Darwin harbor, February 19, 1942. It was like shooting fish in a barrel.

launched its planes at Darwin. The carrier-based air armada was joined by land-based aircraft from Kendari. Together they soon dispelled any lingering doubt among the retreating Allies that the Australian port might still be used as a secure base of operations.

There was no radar installation at Darwin and the first enemy planes were not detected until they were observed on their attack approach. There were a number of ships in the harbor and for the Japanese it must have been like shooting fish in a barrel. An ammunition ship at the pier was blown sky-high, taking a neighboring troopship with it. The U.S. destroyer *Peary* was hit five times by bombs but went down only after a courageous fight. Tankers, transports, cargo vessels, and small combatants were sunk, damaged, and beached in Darwin harbor that day. By the time the attack had ended, a dozen ships had been sent to the bottom, piers and warehouses had been destroyed, the airfield was demolished, and the town was in flames. The venerable old seaplane tender *Preston* had managed to get under way when the first wave of enemy planes arrived, and although hit she somehow managed to stay afloat. Three of her PBY aircraft which had been moored on the water, however, were destroyed. One other aircraft was out on patrol.

That morning at about 0800 Lieutenant Thomas H. Moorer and his crew had taken off on a patrol toward Ambon in 22-P-18. As they proceeded north past Melville Island they spotted an unidentified merchantman and decided to check him out. As they approached the ship, nine Japanese fighters dove out of the sun to attack the low-flying Catalina. These were part of a much larger formation of some seventy or more aircraft bound for Darwin.

The first pass by the fighters holed the fuel tanks, knocked out the port engine, and set the Cat afire. Unable to turn the aircraft into the wind, Moorer had no choice but to execute a downwind landing while still under the unrelenting enemy attack. As he remembered it later, "Small balls of fire were bouncing around inside the mechanic's and radio compartment and noise caused by bullets striking the plane was terrific." The copilot, Ensign Walter H. Mosley, had received a head wound during the initial attack and was bleeding profusely. Nevertheless, Mosley jockeyed the throttle on the one good engine while Moorer wrestled with the yoke. The problem of getting the big airplane down in one piece was compounded by the fact that the float-extension mechanism had been shot away and there were no wing-tip floats to stabilize the aircraft on the water during the landing run out. Because of the unbalanced condition of the Catalina caused by the dead engine, Moorer would have to fight to keep the plane level, and prevent a wing tip from digging into a wave and

38

sending the stricken Cat careening across the water like a flaming pinwheel.

Due to the abnormally higher speed of a downwind approach the PBY hit the water with a resounding smack and bounced three times before coming to a stop. By this time the port waist gun had been abandoned because of the fire on that side; but Aviation Ordnanceman Second Class T. R. LeBaron hung on to the starboard gun and continued firing at the enemy aircraft despite the searing heat. Other crew members broke out one of the large rubber life rafts and found to their consternation that it had been riddled with bullets. A second raft was inflated and it proved to be more serviceable. This was none too soon, because the after section of the plane had begun to melt from the intense heat of the gasoline-fed fire. The enemy fighters left the burning Catalina to its fate and departed to the south looking for bigger game.

Tom Moorer and his crew were adrift only a short time before they were picked up by the Philippine merchant vessel *Florence D.*, which they had earlier sought to investigate. The ship, under charter to the U.S. Navy to run supplies and ammunition to the defenders of Corregidor, had seen the one-sided air battle and come to the rescue. Once aboard, the wounded were treated and all received a meal and a change of clothes. Meanwhile the *Florence D.* turned and headed for Darwin.

About 1500 that afternoon the old freighter was spotted and attacked by dive bombers from the Japanese strike force. After two direct hits which doomed the ship, Moorer ordered his crew over the side and into the water. The dive bombers continued to pound the *Florence D.*, which soon went down by the bow. Fortunately, two of the ship's lifeboats survived the attack and proceeded to pick up survivors. All but one of the PBY crew members made it.

Since the ship's captain had been severely wounded, Tom Moorer took command of the situation. Stationing himself in one boat and Ensign Mosley in the other, they hoisted sails and made for Bathurst Island, arriving shortly after dark and negotiating a successful landing through the surf. There on the 21st they attracted the attention of an RAAF aircraft and were rescued the following morning by an Australian sub-chaser. In the early hours of the 23rd they arrived at Darwin to find the city demolished and virtually deserted. The *Preston*, though damaged in the Darwin attack, was still operational and returned to retrieve Moorer and his crew on the 25th.[6]

If things were bad at Darwin they were even worse elsewhere. The Japanese pressed on relentlessly and to the Allied defenders it was almost as if the world was coming apart at the seams. Indeed for some it was. On Java, where the Dutch had ruled since the early part of the seventeenth century and where generations of Dutch had been born and raised, the unthinkable was about to happen. There was simply no way that Dutch forces, even with help from their American, British, and Australian allies, could withstand the Japanese onslaught. Java too had to fall.

The naval base at Surabaja had already been pounded into rubble. Enemy planes now arrived daily during daylight hours to bomb and strafe in an attempt to neutralize any remaining forces which still might offer resistance to the inevitable invasion of Java. The PBYs of PATWING 10 based at Surabaja were obliged to take off in the morning and return after dark to avoid being caught on the surface. Three had already been dispatched to Broome, Australia, in preparation for the evacuation that everyone knew was not far off. Still, operations continued from Surabaja and the PATWING 10 War Diary tells a grim story. It reports that on February 24 PBY number 42 located a Japanese surface force anchored at enemy held Makassar. These would no doubt be part of the invasion force which would soon push south against Java. Plane number 42 was ordered to attack the transports, which it did, scoring only a near-miss. Shortly afterward it reported: "Am being attacked by aircraft north. Many planes in fleet." The War Diary finally notes in an almost resigned manner, reflecting the harsh conditions under which the pilots and crews of PATWING 10 operated, that "Plane #42 did not return to base and is presumed lost." Subsequent extracts from the last days at Surabaja tell of the continuing struggle by men who already knew how it must end:

25 February—Plane #5 reported "Am being attacked by fighters 0235." Escaped from this attack. COMPATWING 10 reported #44 did not return from patrol today.

26 February—No patrols today as there are no planes available. Of the 3 at Surabaja, 1 will not be ready to fly tomorrow morning. The second can fly but has no radio. Commander in Chief Asiatic Fleet has radio from this plane. This plane will fly personnel out of Surabaja to Broome, then remain south. The third plane can fly but has radio receiver only and floats cannot be raised or lowered. Of the 3 planes at Broome, 2 are badly in need of engines but can fly. The third one is good and will proceed to Surabaja tomorrow.

27 February—At 0940 26 enemy bombers in 3 waves made attacks on the Navy Yard. Plane #5 departed on night patrol, Lt. (j.g.) Hoffman; #3 Lt. Hyland departed at 2200 for Australia with 17 passengers."[7]

Catalina on the step. At Surabaja PBYs took off at dawn and returned at dusk to avoid being caught on the ground. (U.S. Navy)

It was also on the 27th that the seaplane tender *Langley,* in an attempt to bring in thirty-two P-40E fighters for the defense of Java, was intercepted and sunk by Japanese aircraft.* This was also the date of the Battle of the Java Sea where a relatively small force of Allied ships under the command of Dutch Admiral Doorman steamed forth from Surabaja to make a brave but unsuccessful stand against vastly superior Japanese naval forces, in a last-ditch attempt to prevent the invasion of Java. Several Allied ships, including the U.S. cruiser *Houston,* were lost in the fighting. On the night of February 28 the enemy began to land troops on the north coast of Java. The PBYs, staying one jump ahead of the Japanese, retreated to Tjilatjap, the only significant deep-water port on the southern coast of the doomed island. They were joined there by PBYs from Broome which had flown north to assist in the evacuation. It was here that the overworked starboard engine on Lieutenant John Hyland's

*The coup de grace was actually administered by USS *Whipple* after it had been determined that the *Langley* could not be saved.

41

plane number 3 ceased to function, necessitating abandonment of the aircraft. At the end of the day on March 2, Captain Frank Wagner departed Tjilatjap on the last American Catalina out of Java. Altogether, it was an inglorious departure, with native and Dutch civilians watching in disbelief as their world collapsed around them.

The *Childs* was waiting at Broome for the PBYs, but even this Australian port located over 700 miles to the southwest would prove to be no sanctuary. On March 3, Japanese aircraft attacked Broome and destroyed two of the newly arrived PBYs on the water. The crews of these aircraft suffered no casualties, but several civilian refugees were killed or wounded aboard Dutch flying boats also moored there.

PATWING 10 was now virtually extinct. Almost all of the forty-five aircraft which had become part of the inventory since December 7 had met violent ends, and a number had taken their crews with them. Yet, contrary to popular belief, PATWING 10 did not cease to exist. Reduced to only three airplanes, it continued to operate from southwest Australia and survived during this period to fight again another day. Later, the Cats of VP-101, with some of the original pilots and crewmen who endured those desperate days of retreat and humiliation, would return to the fray to repay the enemy.

But during the spring of 1942 one more spectacular and courageous act was performed by the indomitable Cat crews of PATWING 10 which deserves to be told. Bataan had fallen and the end was near for the island bastion of Corregidor. By the last part of April, the stubborn defenders had almost exhausted their supplies of food, medical supplies, and ammunition with which to carry on the fight. Worse still, they were almost entirely cut off from their countrymen, who had been obliged to retreat all the way to Australia. The airfield on the tiny island was too small to accommodate large long-range bombers of the Army Air Force, and smaller aircraft simply could not negotiate the distance. Large numbers of enemy aircraft frequented the Corregidor area by day, and natural hazards combined with deadly Japanese artillery to make the mission only slightly less hazardous at night. Nevertheless, the Navy was asked to attempt one last flight employing the special characteristics of the Catalinas to maximum advantage.

Two Cats took off from Perth, Australia at 1000 on the morning of April 27, 1942, and flew north to Sharks Bay. There they were refueled by the faithful old *William B. Preston* and sent on their way. Lieutenant Commander Edgar Neale, who was in overall command of the mission, flew in number 1 piloted by Lieutenant (j.g.) Thomas F. Pollock and Naval Aviation Pilot (NAP) D. W. Bounds. The second aircraft, number 7, was flown by Lieutenants (j.g.) Leroy Deede and William Gough, with NAP W. D. Eddy as third pilot. These men were being asked to do nothing less than to fly their vulnerable old Catalinas deep into Japanese-held territory, make hazardous night landings under the guns of the enemy, offload heavy cargoes, and fly back to safety with a large number of passengers. These pilots and crew members were mostly young men with relatively limited experience, but their demonstrated ability to survive in "Cold Turkey Alley" over the past few months had made them combatwise beyond their years. It was thought that they just might be able to pull it off.

At about 0600 on the 28th, after an all-night flight along the Australian coast, the two Catalinas arrived at Darwin where they would pick up ammunition, radio parts, and medical supplies for the battered defenders of Corregidor. Because the Australian port was now subject to almost daily enemy air attack, the planes refueled hurriedly and retired to a sheltered area on a river some miles from the city, where the Japanese bombers were unlikely to find them. Later in the day they returned to Darwin to load their cargoes. Neale had everything ready and waiting and they were soon ready to depart. Now the trick would be to thread their way north through Japanese-held territory which bristled with enemy bases, ships, patrol planes, antiaircraft batteries, and deadly Zero fighters. It went without saying that such an audacious undertaking could only be accomplished at night—maybe. The fall of Corregidor was imminent, and this would be the last flight to the besieged island fortress. They had to try.

Heavily laden, the Cats departed Darwin at 1630 that afternoon on a heading of 320 degrees, timed to arrive off the island of Timor after dark. Their calculations placed them there at the appointed time and as they moved slowly northwest into the Banda Sea, they wondered if they had been seen and whether Japanese fighters based at Dili might now be scrambling into the night sky to intercept them. Nothing like that happened, and as they moved further into the covering darkness over the ocean they began to feel that they had not been observed.

At position 05° 00′ S, 24° 30′ W, they turned north for a straight shot at their destination, continuing past the Japanese air bases at Kendari to the west and Ambon somewhat further to the east without incident. A good position check was obtained at Taliabu and they now proceeded to the next possible trouble spot, the city of Manado far out on the long finger of land which projects eastward from Celebes Island. Here the two Cats passed within fifteen miles of the Japanese stronghold which Tom Pollock described as being "lit up like a Christmas tree." From there they flew north into the Celebes Sea, where they were able to relax briefly before coming upon the island of Mindanao, the large southern island in the Philippine archipelago.

Davao, at the northwestern corner of Davao Gulf, was another enemy hot spot, so to avoid detection the two aircraft skirted that part of the big island, made their way up into the Moro Gulf, and finally made a turn to the northwest for a short leg over land to Lake Lanao. This was to be their jumping-off point for Corregidor and there they found a light blinking through the darkness just as they had been briefed. After an exchange of recognition signals, the planes began their let-down into the darkness below.

A slick flat surface can play dangerous tricks on the eyes and many a hairy water landing can be attributed to this phenomenon. During daylight hours this sort of distorted depth perception is rarely a problem because the pilot usually has surface objects for reference, such as a tree line, a small craft, or even a buoy. At night, though, especially without benefit of landing lights or lighted sea-lane buoys, the problem is greatly magnified. The sensation is that of descending into a black pit not knowing what one might find at the bottom. But despite the very real possibility of running headlong into a darkened vessel, a partially submerged reef, or a floating log, such landings were frequently required of

Lieutenant Thomas F. Pollock (far right) and his crew were awarded Silver Stars for their flight to Corregidor. (Rear Admiral T. A. Christopher collection)

Cat crews operating in the western Pacific when circumstances warranted. This was one of those times.

There was no way to accurately determine wind direction on the surface of the lake, so Tom Pollock made his best guess, established a heading, and set up a steady rate of descent. The copilot went over the remaining items on the checklist and scanned the inky blackness outside the aircraft to no avail. In the glare of the instrument lights they watched the altimeter wind down slowly. When it registered three hundred feet, Pollock began to ease back on the yoke to slow the rate of descent. Then when the aircraft reached the desired airspeed he simply held that attitude until the hull made firm contact with the surface. In effect, he had driven the aircraft onto the water. Back came the throttles and the big boat quickly slowed to taxi speed. This technique, properly executed, results in a harder landing than the customary full-flare touchdown, but it is infinitely safer under these conditions. Leroy Deede, using the same technique landed shortly afterward, also without incident. So far, so good.

A native boat was waiting for them and led the two Catalinas to separate hiding places along the shore. Maneuvering the big boats into their assigned niches was precarious in the darkness, but in a relatively short time they were tied up under the trees. There they were camouflaged further with brush and freshly cut jungle foliage, making discovery from the air all but impossible. All hands worked at this task until after daylight, at which time the pilots and crewmen, satisfied that the PBYs were adequately hidden, tried to get some sleep. The planes' arrival, however, had attracted a number of natives who quickly transformed the occasion into something of a social event. The noise and activity around the aircraft made sleep almost impossible.

By late afternoon the Cats had been refueled and checked over carefully for the last and most hazardous leg of the flight to Corregidor. More cargo was stowed aboard and to compensate for the extra weight the aircraft were stripped of all "non-essential" equipment. Pollock later remarked that when they removed the .50-caliber waist guns, "It was like parting with old friends. . . ."

Takeoff time was at 1845 that night. The two PBYs broke water on schedule and headed west down a valley with mountains rising on each side. By the time they reached the west coast of Mindanao it was dark and they headed northwest into the Sulu Sea. Most of the flight was flown over water so the enemy would have the least possible opportunity to detect them. They checked their navigation at selected islands as they proceeded along course and finally passed over Lubang Island, only 50 miles from their destination.

Corregidor is a natural island fortress which rises abruptly from the sea at the entrance to Manila Bay. Here Lieutenant General Jonathan Wainwright and a courageous group of American and Filipino fighting men had held out against numerically overwhelming enemy forces for four months. From tunnels carved deep into the rock they endured merciless air and artillery bombardment which made the ground quake almost continually during the long hours under attack, to such an extent that men were frequently knocked off their feet as they moved about. Massive arrays of Japanese artillery pieces were positioned on the Bataan Peninsula about two miles to the north and at Cavite Province some six and a half miles to the south. The Cats were instructed to land to the south and east of Corregidor where they were least likely to be spotted. Unfortunately, there was little protection in this area from the swells that rolled in from the South China Sea.

As the PBYs approached Manila Bay they attempted to pick up radio signals from the occupied capital city, but without success. This was of little consequence because it was only a short sprint from Lubang Island and they hit their destination on the nose. Manila, some twenty-eight miles across the bay, was blacked out, but an oil storage tank on Corregidor itself which had been hit by enemy bombardment was burning brightly. This impromptu beacon provided a reference point, wind direction information, and even a little light for the difficult landing. Both planes made it safely onto the water, where they awaited the contact vessel. The darkened boat arrived on the scene a few minutes later. She was much too large to come alongside and smaller boats were employed to shuttle passengers to, and cargo from, the two Catalinas. All were aware that if they were discovered, the enemy guns would make short work of them. But somehow the Japanese seemed asleep at the switch. By coincidence, it was the Emperor's birthday and it is probable that the Japanese artillerymen had relaxed their guard somewhat for this important national day.

Lieutenant (j.g.) Pollock, fully expecting to be fired upon at any moment picked up the mike and said, "After station from pilot—Get those old women aboard and let's get out of here—there is Jap artillery on both sides that can make us very unhappy." To Pollock's surprise several women *had* been put aboard—but they were hardly old and certainly not decrepit. These were Army nurses, ten in all who were being evacuated from "The Rock" on the last flight out. Deede had thirteen nurses aboard his plane. In addition both aircraft carried an assortment of military and civilian personnel, mostly Americans and a few Filipinos. "One boat" had picked up twenty-five passengers while "Seven boat" had taken aboard thirty. They were all moved as far forward as possible and full power was applied for the takeoff run. The two planes, which now rode low in the water from the excess weight, plunged forward into the choppy sea, sending up clouds of spray and creating temporary instrument conditions until they were airborne. Both planes made the takeoff successfully despite the adverse conditions and climbed slowly into the night sky. There was more than one sigh of relief as they headed out into the South China Sea. The coffee pot was turned on almost immediately and was kept active throughout the flight.

At about the halfway mark on the return flight to Lake Lanao they began to encounter clouds. A short time later the two planes became separated and each proceeded on its own. Upon arrival at the lake, Pollock found a hole in the cloud cover and made the tricky night landing, again without incident. Deede found a solid overcast over the landing area and decided not to add bad weather to an already risky undertaking. Instead he proceeded to the coast where the cloud cover had begun to dissipate and landed in a sheltered bay. At first light he took off and proceeded to Lake Lanao. Both planes were camouflaged as before, refueled for the flight south, and then left to await the cover of darkness.

At about 1800 the Cats were ready. Leroy Deede in "Seven boat" was the first out of his hiding place and circled in the open water as he checked his engines and waited for the lead plane. But "One boat" had difficulty getting clear of the shore and in the process of being towed into a position where the engines could be started, struck a submerged reef which did considerable damage to the hull. Pollock quickly started the engines and taxied the wounded Cat back to the beach so that she would not sink in deep water. By this time it was quite dark and he signalled to Deede with his aldis lamp to go on. "Seven boat" acknowledged the order and departed.

Now began a herculean effort to refloat and repair the torn aircraft. With the help of empty fuel drums, she was raised to a position where she could be worked on. A diver located the holes and reported that one was quite large. It was questionable whether it could be repaired but there seemed to be no more reasonable alternative than to try. There was considerable incentive to get the old Cat back in flying condition again because the Japanese had made a successful landing on the coast of Mindanao only thirty-seven miles away and the Lake Lanao refuge was expected to fall into their hands in the very near future. All night and most of the next day they worked to devise a crude patch using a blanket, part of a tree trunk and some marine glue. Late that afternoon they were ready to try to get the battered craft into the air.

There was still some water in the aircraft and they would probably take on more when they taxied out. Because of the extra weight it had

47

been determined that no more than ten passengers could be taken along but a B-17 had been ordered in to a nearby field to pick up those remaining behind. Cautiously they towed the plane into open water and started the engines. As the Catalina moved forward under her own power the water began to pour in around the patch at a great rate and Pollock knew that it was now or never. There was no time to warm up the engines or to check the magnetos. He simply applied full throttle and the plane, with several thousand pounds of water sloshing around the hull, began its takeoff run. After what seemed like an eternity the Cat lifted itself up and onto the step and allowed Pollock to coax her into the air. They staggered along just above stalling speed but they were airborne. Slowly the water began to drain out and the Cat began to act like her old self again. Now to thread their way back to Australia via the unfriendly skies of Cold Turkey Alley.

As it turned out, the flight back to Darwin was uneventful. The Japanese strongholds slipped beneath them during the night without any sign that they had been detected. The exhausted Cat crew and their harried passengers landed at Darwin the next morning and kept the plane afloat by bailing furiously until she was refueled. Then they took off for Perth, flying this remaining leg in a straight line across the northwestern corner of the great continent. Landing at their destination at 0130 on the morning of May 3, 1942, they drove the leaking aircraft up onto the beach to prevent it from sinking.

The success of this mission was marred only by the fact that no B-17 was able to make it into Mindanao to evacuate the passengers and other personnel who had remained behind at Lake Lanao. They were later captured and imprisoned by the Japanese. Corregidor itself fell to the enemy on May 6. But the round-trip flight of the two Catalinas was a spectacular achievement for which each of the crew members who participated was awarded the Silver Star. No long-range land plane could have accomplished the feat. It was a job for slow, surefooted, and skillfully flown Cats. And it was a job that could only have been carried off successfully in the kind of environment in which feline creatures perform best—the black of night.[8]

4

Guts Ball

The Americans and their allies were being mauled in the Southwest Pacific and there was no relief in sight. The Japanese, on the other hand, had enjoyed phenomenal success from the very beginning and it must have seemed to them that their efforts were indeed sanctioned by divine providence. Although their plans to invade Port Moresby in southeastern New Guinea were frustrated at the Battle of the Coral Sea, this was considered no more than a temporary setback. After all, they had sunk the aircraft carrier *Lexington*, an oiler, and a destroyer in that engagement, and had seriously damaged the carrier *Yorktown* as well.* Moreover, they had taken the island of Tulagi in the Solomon Islands on May 4 as planned. From there they intended to continue their expansion southward as far as New Caledonia, Fiji, and Samoa, thereby completing an island barrier which would separate Australia from its American ally.

In Japan, still further plans had been set in motion to extend the defense perimeter northeast to the Aleutians and across the Pacific to Midway Island. After that was accomplished there would be no more Doolittle-type raids on the homeland, and on the offensive side of the coin, Hawaii itself might even be invaded. It was heady stuff!

The time had also come to deal a final crushing blow to the remnants of U.S. seapower in the Pacific. Admiral Isoroku Yamamoto clearly had this in mind when his armada sallied forth from Japan and the Marianas during the last days of May 1942. Altogether it was an impressive array

---

*The Japanese lost the light carrier *Shoho* while the larger carrier *Shokaku* sustained considerable damage.

*Admiral Isoroku Yamamoto. His powerful forces converged
on Midway for a decisive naval showdown (U.S. Navy)*

of naval might, numbering close to two hundred vessels and including eight aircraft carriers, eleven battleships, and a variety of other combatants, transports, and support ships. Almost one-quarter of this force, including two light carriers, was dispatched to the north for the Aleutian operation. The remainder of the fleet was earmarked for the showdown at Midway. Admiral Nobutake Kondo, Commander-in-Chief of the Japanese Second Fleet, was to join transports and other supporting units from Guam and Saipan and approach Midway from the southwest. Meanwhile the carrier striking force under Admiral Nagumo was to fall upon the island outpost from the northwest. The Commander-in-Chief of the combined fleet, Admiral Yamamoto in the super-battleship *Yamato*, followed some distance behind the striking force with the main body.

The Americans for their part could muster no battleships and only three aircraft carriers to defend Midway. One of the carriers, the *Yorktown*, which had been damaged at the Battle of the Coral Sea, had only three days in dry dock where temporary repairs were hastily made to enable her to participate in the historic struggle. Counting support vessels and submarines, the American force numbered only about fifty ships in all. On the plus side, however, they had the advantage of land-based aircraft which could seek out the approaching fleet at more than twice the range of enemy carrier-based planes. But most important

50

of all, the Americans had broken the Japanese code and knew they were coming. What they did not know was the exact size of the enemy fleet, how it would be deployed against Midway, or precisely when and where it would make its appearance.

The American force was positioned to the northeast of Midway because it was believed that the Japanese approach would be from the northwest. It was to be an ambush and Pat Bellinger had put together an ambitious search plan for his PBYs to locate the enemy ships early in the game. He calculated that the Japanese would try to repeat their performance at Pearl Harbor and that their carriers would attempt to arrive within launching distance of Midway in the early-morning hours. His plan, therefore, called for deployment of twenty-four PBYs to operate from the tiny island base, each plane covering a sector eight degrees in width and seven hundred miles long. This provided coverage in an arc stretching more that 180 degrees clockwise from south to north. With luck they would detect the enemy a day before the attack. On May 30 he put this plan into operation.

Bellinger, of course, was well aware of the vulnerability of his Catalinas to fighter attack and advised Admiral Chester A. Nimitz, Commander-in-Chief of the U.S. Pacific Fleet, that they should not be used in a daylight offensive role. But he pointed out that they might be loaded with torpedoes and employed effectively as attack aircraft at night. "Torpedo attacks," he said, "[should] be driven home with determination to close range—every torpedo drop a hit."[1] It was no easy undertaking, to be sure, and Pat Bellinger knew that what he was suggesting as a kind of afterthought was guts ball. A night aerial torpedo attack against a real enemy had never been attempted before by the U.S. Navy. But this was a battle that could well decide the course of the war in the Pacific. If the Cats could make any kind of a meaningful contribution it was worth a try.

On the morning of June 3 Ensign Jack Reid and his crew had arrived at the outermost limit of their search sector. Instead of turning, however, he elected to continue on just a bit further. It was well he did because a few minutes later the Catalina came upon a formation of enemy ships bound for Midway. What he had discovered was part of the occupation force, but the young plane commander mistook it for the striking force and radioed back to base that they had located the "main body."

That afternoon, nine B-17 Flying Fortresses of the Army Air Corps were sent out to make high-altitude bombing attacks on the enemy task force which was approaching from the southwest. The attack was unsuccessful although the pilots mistakenly thought they had scored hits on two warships and two transports. It was yet to be learned that high-altitude bombing was, in most cases, ineffective against underway surface vessels.

Also on that afternoon four amphibious-type PBY-5As were flown in from Pearl Harbor to try their luck. None of the pilots knew what was happening at Midway nor were they told about the task that lay before them. Lieutenant (j.g.) Charlie Hibberd, plane commander of 24-P-12, remembers his arrival on Eastern Island, one of the two tiny sandbar islands of the Midway Atoll.* "It was not until we reached Midway," he recalls, "that we realized something important was going on." The island was "a veritable beehive of activity."[2] No sooner had the planes taxied into their parking spaces than ordnancemen began hanging live torpedoes under the wings. For the plane crews, which had already been in the air for ten hours, this was certainly an unexpected development. As the pilots climbed down to the ground they were hustled away to a briefing where their curiosity was quickly satisfied.

They were told that an enemy force, steaming in two columns, had been located that morning to the west of Midway at a distance of about 700 miles. There were cruisers, destroyers, transports, and an aircraft carrier in the formation, the briefing officer said. Captain Simard, Commanding Officer of the Naval Air Station, gave it to them bluntly. They were going to launch four PBYs "on a volunteer basis," he said. Lieutenant W. L. "Red" Richards would lead the flight in Hibberd's aircraft. "The other volunteers," he said with a grim smile, "will be Mr. Propst, Mr. Davis, and that little Ensign in the back there," nodding at Ensign Alan Rothenberg. "That was the first we realized," Rothenberg says, "what was in store for us."[3] Then they went back to the aircraft, arriving just in time to see the ordnance crews finish their work.

Each of the Cats had been loaded with a 2,200-pound Mark XIII, Mod 1 aircraft-launched torpedo. These weapons had entered into service in 1938 but had not been adequately tested and evaluated prior to the Pearl Harbor attack. At the time of the Battle of Midway there had still been little opportunity to use the Mark XIII under actual combat conditions. The pilots of the carrier-based torpedo bombers would soon discover that this weapon left much to be desired.

The basic problem was one of transition from an air to a water environment. It was difficult to control the drop angle and consequently the water entry and the sensitive inner mechanisms which regulated the performance of the torpedo were often thrown askew by the jarring

*Eastern Island is the smaller of the two land masses at Midway with most of its area taken up by runways. The other is Sand Island, which served as a seaplane base. Since the four Catalinas in question were amphibians, it was more convenient to load and service them at Eastern Island.

Midway. Eastern Island is in the foreground. (U.S. Navy)

impact. To be effective, the Mark XIII had to be dropped from an altitude of no more that sixty feet at a speed which made the delivery aircraft an easy target for antiaircraft gunners or fighters. In wartime, this type of approach was not conducive to longevity. But even when these limitations were strictly observed, the Mark XIII displayed tendencies to swerve to the left or run at the wrong depth. Some time later, in the summer of 1943, after several improvements, 105 of these torpedoes were evaluated following drops at speeds in excess of 150 knots. According to the Bureau of Ordnance, "36 percent ran cold, 20 percent sank, 20 percent had poor deflection performance, 2 percent ran on the surface, and only 31 percent gave a satisfactory run."[4] But in the spring of 1942 the Mark XIII was the only air-launched torpedo available.

Charlie Hibberd remembers having had some previous experience with dummy torpedoes and he knew how to operate the torpedo "gunsight." This somewhat primitive device, officially known as a torpedo director, was mounted on the center line of the aircraft just above the

53

PBY cockpit. The arrows show the manual release handles used for dropping weapons manually. (U.S. Navy)

instrument panel. There it could be used by either the pilot or the copilot, depending upon the perspective from which the target vessel was approached. Target angles off the port side of the aircraft could best be sighted by the copilot, while the pilot had the optimum view for aiming points on the starboard side. The sight used inputs of torpedo speed (33.5 knots), distance to the target at the time of drop, and estimated target speed. These values were set into the instrument and the target ship was then held fixed in the sight until the drop point was reached and the pilot released the torpedo. The weapon was dropped electrically from the cockpit by means of a firing key, but there were also two manual-release handles, one for the weapons mounted under the wing on each side.

The flight departed Midway at about 2115. With Richards and Hibberd at the controls, 24-P-12 showed its formation and tail lights so the others who were flying in a darkened condition would have a reference point on which to position themselves. Lieutenant (j.g.) D. C. "Doug" Davis in 24-P-7 joined up in loose formation while Ensign G. D. "Dagwood" Propst in 24-P-11 followed somewhat further behind. Al Rothenberg, the junior plane commander in the formation, had difficulty getting off in 51-P-5.

The boarding ladder had jammed in its mounts outside the aircraft and could not be disengaged. Concerned lest he be left behind, Rothenberg ordered a crewman to break the fittings. By the time 51-P-5 got airborne, the other three aircraft were out of sight. Because only the lead plane was showing lights and all were exercising radio silence, Richards was not immediately aware that he was one aircraft short. Rothenberg and his crew proceeded independently to intercept the approaching enemy force.

The pilots had been told to expect contact with the Japanese about 500 miles out. It would be several hours before they reached this position, and considerably longer since the task force had last been sighted. If the enemy had altered course or changed speed the Catalinas might well be obliged to conduct a fuel-consuming search. When and if the enemy was found, the low-level attack at high power settings would mean increased fuel consumption as would the getaway phase, especially if they were pursued by fighters. Accordingly all the planes leaned out shortly after takeoff to save as much precious avgas as possible.

It was a beautiful moonlit night. Billowy white cumulus clouds were scattered throughout the area, with bases at a thousand feet and rising to three thousand or more in places. The Cats cruised on top, occasionally penetrating the upper portions of the clouds. At about midnight, the radar operator on 24-P-12 reported a lone ship off to port. It could have been an enemy picket but it could just as well have been a friendly merchant. Whatever the case the Cats were after bigger game and Richards elected to hold his course. A little over an hour later at 0115 radar reported "about ten ships" again off to port at ten to twelve miles. As they turned toward the ships Hibberd spotted them visually. There they were, just as advertised, steaming in two neat columns toward Midway.

Richards took over the controls and led the planes gingerly around to the down-moon side of the enemy fleet. There were only two aircraft now, Propst having become separated from the group in the darkness and Rothenberg still trailing some distance behind. As the Cats circled for the attack they eased slowly down toward the surface of the water with engines throttled back and all lights extinguished. The enemy ships continued to steam as before, completely unaware of approaching air-craft. Richards selected the last ship in the northernmost column as his intended victim. At that distance he could not identify its type but it presented a larger silhouette than the others and he hoped it might possibly be a carrier. At this point he turned the controls over to Hibberd.

The run-in to the target was made from slightly abaft the port beam. Hibberd was now skimming over the surface at a speed just over one hundred knots. Recalling this memorable event he says:

In practice it's one thing. If you miss you try again. But I did not come all this way to miss with the only torpedo I had. So I kept resetting the sight, all the time charging in closer. I guess I must have reset as quickly as possible about four times before I finally decided that I was close enough to get a hit."[5]

There was no enemy fire. The Japanese had been taken completely by surprise.

As they approached the 800-yard mark Richards barked "Drop the damned thing. . . ."[6] Hibberd hit the firing key and the weapon left the aircraft. "As I pulled the plane up and over what turned out to be a big transport ship we could see men start to rush around on deck and in a few moments my rear gunner let out a whoop that there was a big flash. 'We got a hit' he said. I have always wondered whether that was actually true. . . ."[7] Hibberd knew the reputation of the Mark XIII torpedo and suspected that at night gunfire might easily be mistaken for a hit.

Davis who was not far behind had now begun his run but was dissatisfied with the line-up. Like Hibberd, he was acutely aware that he had only one shot so he broke off his attack and retired to the north, climbing back up to about 2,000 feet. In a few minutes he had set up another. gliding approach on the target vessel's port beam. This time the run was complicated when the ship began an evasive turn to starboard, presenting the PBY with a stern aspect. Davis decided not to break off the attack but to bore in as close as possible before he dropped his weapon. At 200 yards he released his torpedo, added full power, and pulled up sharply over the stern of the enemy vessel. As he did so, his quarry and all the other ships in the vicinity opened fire on him. Davis' port waist gunner strafed the deck of the target vessel as they went by but there was no indication that the torpedo had scored a hit.

At about this time Dagwood Propst, who had been separated from the flight some time earlier, came upon the scene. Chief Aviation Pilot Benny Smathers flew copilot in the right seat. Making a wide spiral turn, Propst chose a large ship near the end of one column and set up his run on the vessel's port quarter. With frequent glances at the altimeter, he eased the big plane closer and closer to the water to get a good water-entry angle on the cranky Mark XIII. The ship made no evasive maneuvers.

Aboard the tanker *Akebono Maru* there was some confusion as to just what was happening. Low-flying aircraft were attacking ships in the formation and there was a lot of wild firing into the air. The planes were making their runs from down-moon and they could not be seen. Where had they come from? There were no known U.S. carriers in this area.

Pilots who flew on the night torpedo mission at Midway. Left to right: Davis, Rothenberg, Richards, and Propst. (U.S. Navy)

Midway was still 550 miles away. Only large land-based multi-engine aircraft could negotiate that distance and make it home again. But these intruders seemed to have the agility of torpedo planes, skimming dangerously close to the surface of the water in the black of night. An officer on the wing of the bridge peered into the darkness off the port side but could see nothing. Then he heard it—the soft hum of throttled down engines. He listened intently. The sound seemed to be getting closer. Too late he turned to shout an order to the helm as a black shape roared overhead. Then there was a blast that shook the ship. The *Akebono Maru* had been hit.

As the Catalina pulled up after torpedo release, enemy antiaircraft guns opened up on the dim form that flashed by in the night. Some shot at the noise of the engines now straining at full power. It was like fighting blindfolded. Propst feinted to the right and then began a tight left turn. Smathers observed a large detonation and they knew they had scored a hit. Suddenly, as they were making their withdrawal, the Cat was attacked by a single aircraft, probably a floatplane fighter which had been hurriedly launched from one of the ships. Propst made for cloud cover and they did not encounter the fighter again.

Al Rothenberg had not been as fortunate as Propst. Upon reaching the area where the enemy task force ought to be, he searched until he had just enough fuel to make it back to Midway. Then, reluctantly, he headed for home. No rendezvous was attempted following the attack and all four planes proceeded independently, arriving in the vicinity of Midway just after sun-up. As they approached the atoll they were greeted with a broadcast by Midway Radio. "AIR RAID MIDWAY," it blared—"MIDWAY IS NOW UNDERGOING AIR RAID." There was no prudent choice but to make for Lisianski Island, a pre-arranged alternate about two hundred and fifty miles down the Hawaiian chain to the southeast. Aside from the fact that most of the past twenty-four hours had been spent in the air, the necessity to divert was not an unsurmountable problem. All four aircraft still had enough reserve fuel to cope with just such an eventuality. But when they arrived at Lisianski they found themselves in a weather front eighty to a hundred miles wide which obscured the island and made a safe landing impossible. Now there was a question as to whether they had enough fuel to reach Laysan Island, more than a hundred miles further on down the chain. Again there was not much choice. Dagwood Propst was the only one who did not have to concern himself with that problem. His fuel had run out and he set his Cat down in the open sea not far from Lisianski. There he and his crew bobbed about until they were rescued three days later by a Cat from VP-23. The plane, which had been damaged upon landing, was sunk by gunfire.

Doug Davis and his crew made Laysan at 1000 with somewhere between ten to twenty gallons of fuel in the tanks. Richards and Hibberd landed forty-five minutes later, while Rothenberg arrived at 1105, also with a critically low fuel state. Behind them, the clash that has been called the turning point of the war in the Pacific was just beginning to unfold.

The Battle of Midway was primarily, of course, a battle between carrier-based aircraft flown from ships which never made visual contact with one another. When it was over, the enemy had lost four front-line carriers, a heavy cruiser, a destroyer, over two hundred and fifty aircraft, and more than two thousand men. The Japanese had been thwarted in their move to establish a base of operations at Midway from which to punish the Americans further and they had failed to destroy the remnants of the U.S. Pacific Fleet. From that time on things would be different.

The contribution made by the four Catalinas in this historic battle was relatively modest in terms of damage inflicted on the enemy. But this night torpedo attack, first of its kind attempted by the U.S. Navy, illustrated the feasibility of the concept and suggested a new and more aggressive role for the much maligned PBYs. Rear Admiral Raymond A. Spruance, Commander of Task Force 16 and hero of the Battle of Midway, noted the historical significance of the event in his endorsement of Richards' report. He also pointed out that:

> The initial contact, and subsequent success of the attack, were in large measure made possible by the radar installation. Night torpedo attack, employing radar, represents one of the few profitable offensive uses of our patrol seaplanes.[8]

Now the idea had to be expanded upon and developed into a useful tactical tool in the long fight that lay ahead.

5

The Black Cat Flies Tonight

Man clearly functions best in daylight. In prehistoric times he rarely ventured forth at night, for he had too many powerful enemies who would make a meal of him. Instead, when darkness came he scurried to the relative safety of some cave or crevice to hide from or fend off the terrifying nocturnal beasts that roamed the earth. Darkness is still a period of anxiety and uncertainty for man. At night, especially in time of danger, fear becomes exaggerated and the imagination works overtime.

This human frailty can be turned to military advantage. A well-executed night attack can have a devastating effect on an ill-prepared defending force. The idea has long been understood as it applies to ground forces, and the Japanese Navy was in the forefront of its development for night surface engagements. In preparation for their struggle with the United States, great emphasis was given to realistic night exercises and this sharpened capability served the Japanese well on a number of occasions.

But night attacks by aircraft at sea were virtually unheard of. For one reason, they were thought to be prohibitively dangerous. Violent maneuvers with a horizon obscured by darkness was an invitation to vertigo. Shadows created by clouds and moonlight created false images on the water. Depth perception was significantly impaired and a reliable radio altimeter, known as an "absolute altimeter," had only recently become available. Of course the hazards of low-level night attack could be decreased to some extent by training and sheer nerve. British Swordfish aircraft had proved this in a daring night torpedo attack in Taranto Harbor, Italy on November 11–12, 1940. By the light of air-dropped

60

flares, the British put three Italian battleships out of action, one permanently. Still, despite the success of this operation, there was no rush to make low-level night attacks a matter of routine. Opportunities like the one presented at Taranto were few. On the open sea, the ability to find the enemy at night remained a limiting factor—that is, until the advent of a new electronic device known as radar.

The concept of ship detection by means of reflected radio signals became known in the United States as early as 1922. It was later discovered that the principle could be applied to the detection of aircraft as well, and by 1934 a system had been devised to measure both bearing and distance to the target. A test model installed on the *New York* had proven so successful during Caribbean fleet exercises in 1939 that twenty similar sets were ordered and earmarked for selected ships and stations.

Meanwhile the British had been busy with their own version of the radio reflection phenomenon, and had carried the concept even further than the Americans. By the late 1930s they had developed the first airborne radar system, which was successfully employed in the Battle of Britain against the Luftwaffe. By October 1940 they had also produced the first operational Air-To-Surface Vessel (ASV) radar. It was not long before the two allies were cooperating fully in the use of the important new technology. By the summer of 1941 a U.S. Navy squadron of Martin PBM-1 Mariners was outfitted with British ASV radar systems for anti-submarine patrol operations out of Iceland. By early 1942 the United States had its own model in operation and began installing some of these sets in PBY Catalinas. Now the Cats had eyes that could see in the dark.*

The Japanese were aware of American and British research in the field of radio detection. Indeed, Japanese scientists had themselves been working on the problem since 1936 and although they had received somewhat less than enthusiastic support from military circles, a primitive stationary model was in use by 1939. But in the euphoria of early victories over Allied forces, the development of radar took a back seat. Some Japanese military leaders seemed to regard radio detection as a defensive concept which was somehow unworthy of the Japanese fighting spirit. In any case, the progress of the war had shown little need for such a device against the soft-willed Americans. It was believed that any technological advantage the Allies might derive from their innovations could certainly be offset by the demonstrated superiority of the Japanese fighting man who had been trained for combat under adverse weather conditions, as well as in total darkness. As a result of this incredible attitude, the Japanese never produced a really effective operational

*Early ASV radar was very primitive by today's standards. It operated in the 187 megahertz range with simple fixed "Yagi" antennae on the wings.

Shadows born of clouds and moonlight create false images, and a horizon obscured by darkness is an invitation to vertigo. (U.S. Navy)

radar. They would pay dearly for their failure to recognize the significance of this new device until it was too late.

As has already been noted, the Japanese had landed on the island of Tulagi in the Solomons in early May 1942 and had established a seaplane base on the small adjacent island of Gavatu. This was in preparation for further moves down the Solomon chain toward New Caledonia, Fiji, and Samoa. But the shattering American victory at Midway caused them to take a close, hard look at their plans in this area. They decided that immediate emphasis would be given to the conquest of Port Moresby. This time, however, they would land their troops on the northeast coast of New Guinea and march them over the Owen Stanley mountains to their objective on the southern shore. Plans for a major move south by way of the Solomons were relegated to a back burner for the moment. But the seaplane base at Tulagi would be helpful in protecting their eastern flank from a surprise American thrust from that direction.

The Americans, on the other hand, had begun to think about an offensive of their own in this part of the world. General MacArthur originally thought that an attack could be launched directly against the Japanese stronghold at Rabaul. But this would have been a formidable and ill-advised undertaking. Navy planners thought it might be better to stage an initial landing on Tulagi and, after securing that area, move up the island chain toward the enemy bastion at Rabaul. On the second of July the Joint Chiefs of Staff made the decision and directed a three-phased effort. First, U.S. forces would seize the Santa Cruz Islands, Tulagi, and adjacent areas, including the large island of Guadalcanal. Next, they would occupy the rest of the Solomon Islands and parts of New Guinea. Finally, they would mount an assault on Rabaul and its surrounding area.

The first phase, seizure of Tulagi, was called "Operation Watchtower." Due to the very limited resources which were then available to prosecute the move, it jokingly, but perhaps somewhat appropriately, became known as "Operation Shoestring" by many of those who were charged with its implementation. Overall command of the operation fell to Vice Admiral Robert L. Ghormley who had just been named Commander, South Pacific Force and Area (COMSOPAC). Land-based aircraft, including the PBYs, were under the command of Rear Admiral John S. McCain, Commander Aircraft South Pacific Area and Commander Task Force 63. He directed his forces from the seaplane tender *Curtiss* located at Nouméa, New Caledonia, and later at Espiritu Santo in the New Hebrides. This latter island would be the main support base for "Operation Watchtower."

In early July it was discovered that the Japanese had begun to build an airfield on Guadalcanal. Admiral Ghormley, who had grave reservations concerning "Watchtower" and the August 1 target date, recommended to CINCPAC that the operation be shelved for the time being until they could muster greater strength. Admiral Ernest J. King, who had become Chief of Naval Operations in March of that year, saw the airfield development as a new imperative to proceed on schedule. If the Japanese were permitted to complete this project they could be expected to use the airfield to continue their drive southward, threatening the U.S. base at Espiritu Santo.

A five-plane detachment made up of PBYs from VP-11 and VP-14, under the command of Lieutenant Jim Cobb, began operating from Ndeni in the Santa Cruz Islands on August 5.

A VP-91 Cat refuels from the tender Mackinac *at Vanikoro Island in the Santa Cruz group, October 1942. (Captain D. Walkinshaw collection)*

The operations order directed us to "seize Ndeni." So we steamed in—five patrol planes—and landed in Graciosa Bay to be tended by USS *McFarland*. That constituted the seizure of Ndeni.[1]

The tender *Mackinac* moved even further north with nine more Catalinas from VP-23, and on the 7th anchored in the estuary between Malaita and Maramasike Islands, only 75 miles east of Tulagi. Planes from the two ships along with others from Espiritu Santo combed the ocean to the north and east of Guadalcanal, searching for enemy forces which might have been sent south to oppose the landing. They found nothing. "Fortunately," said Cobb, "the whole operation was a complete surprise to the Japanese. We ran into almost no opposition except for a few float planes."[2]

The Marines, commanded by Major General Alexander A. Vandegrift, went ashore on the islands of Guadalcanal and Tulagi on August 7, supported by Vice Admiral Frank Jack Fletcher's Task Force 61. By the end of the following day, all objectives of the assault had been secured, including the all-important airfield on Guadalcanal. There the enemy, a large number of whom were construction personnel, simply fell back into the jungle to await reinforcement. On Tulagi and the small adjacent

64

islands of Gavatu and Tanambogo the choice facing the small Japanese garrison was surrender or annihilation. Early on the morning of the 7th the commander radioed his decision to Rabaul. "The enemy force is overwhelming. We will defend our positions to the death."[3] And so they did. Planes of the 25th Air Flotilla were hurriedly dispatched to assist the defenders, but these were effectively countered by Admiral Fletcher's carrier-based aircraft.

The landings were a complete success, but the fighting had just begun. The unexpected American assault at Guadalcanal now threatened Japanese expansion plans, as well as the gains already made. The affront could not go unchallenged. Yet despite the certainty of a Japanese counter-attack Admiral Fletcher chose this time to withdraw his carrier task force to the south, leaving the combatant surface ships of Rear Admiral Richmond Kelly Turner's Amphibious Force to guard the beachhead as well as the transports and cargo vessels still unloading offshore. It was a serious misjudgement.

On the afternoon of August 7, Vice Admiral Gunichi Mikawa in the heavy cruiser *Chokai* sortied from Simpson Harbor at Rabaul with two light cruisers and a destroyer, rendezvousing with four additional cruisers at sea. Then they headed south, proceeding down New Georgia Sound ("the Slot") to arrive at their destination in the early-morning hours of August 9. The Americans were no match for the night-experienced Japanese, and the Battle of Savo Island went badly. The cruisers *Vincennes*, *Astoria*, and *Quincy* were lost, as was the Australian cruiser *Canberra*. The *Chicago* was heavily damaged. Mikawa and his task force steamed north in triumph.

Under the circumstances Admiral Turner had no other reasonable alternative than to withdraw his ships from the area, leaving the Marines in an unenviable position. But this was the first major offensive ground action in the Pacific and the Marines had come to stay. Personnel of the 1st Marine Engineer Battalion quickly went to work and completed the Japanese airstrip, which was subsequently named Henderson Field. A PBY-5A Catalina landed on the 2,600-foot dirt runway on the 12th, and by the 20th, Marine Corps fighters and dive bombers were operating from the field.

After the Battle of Savo Island the Japanese began the practice of reinforcing and resupplying their troops on Guadalcanal by night. Their ships moved down "the Slot" under the cover of darkness to unload their cargoes of men and material and also to bombard Marine positions at Henderson Field before heading north again. By the time the sun came up they were back under the umbrella of land-based air from Rabaul. The recurring nocturnal visits became so routine that they were known as the

"Tokyo Express." The Japanese, very much at home in the night environment, operated with virtual impunity and the U.S. Navy seemed unable to do very much about it.

Later in the month the enemy came south in force for an engagement which has come to be called the Battle of the Eastern Solomons. PBYs from the tender *Mackinac*, moored at Ndeni in the Santa Cruz Islands, located a transport group on the morning of the 23rd but a strike flight of five Catalinas launched that night could not find the approaching Japanese ships again. The next morning a PBY found the carrier *Ryujo* and her escorts. In the battle which followed, planes from the *Saratoga* sank the *Ryujo*. The Japanese also lost a destroyer and suffered heavy damage to other ships. But all this did little to alter the strange operating pattern which was developing. During daylight hours the U.S. Navy ruled the waves in the area around Guadalcanal and brought in supplies and reinforcements under cover of aircraft from Henderson Field. But at night it was an entirely different story. Then the Tokyo Express came down the Slot under cover of night to land their troops and bludgeon the Marines at Henderson with naval gunfire. It was almost as if an agreement existed between the two sides, giving the Americans the day shift and the Japanese the night. And so it continued, throughout September and into October.

Even when there was no bombardment the Marines at Henderson rarely had a good night's sleep. In early October the Japanese began the practice of sending single aircraft to harass the Americans after dark. Although these aircraft rarely did any serious damage, their nightly visits took a toll in terms of fatigue and a chafing of nervous systems. Somehow the Marines retained their sense of humor and the lone Japanese marauder was affectionately dubbed "Washing Machine Charlie."

A naval battle off Savo Island on the 11th and 12th of October, subsequently called the Battle of Cape Esperance, cost the Japanese several ships. Nevertheless, they were able to put troops, heavy field pieces, and supplies ashore. The Americans reinforced the Marines during the daylight hours of the 13th despite some opposition from enemy aircraft and ground artillery. But that night (actually, during the early-morning hours of the 14th), Vice Admiral Takeo Kurita arrived off the island with two battleships and other surface combatants. These behemoths gave Henderson Field a pasting that no one who lived through it ever forgot. The field was pockmarked with craters from the huge 14-inch projectiles and more than half of the American planes were destroyed. The following night the Japanese hit the Marines again, this time with 8-inch guns. The purpose of all this heavy attention was to destroy or immobilize the

The Cats were soon making night raids on Japanese airfields, installations, and troop positions as a matter of routine. (U.S. Navy)

aircraft at Henderson and to make the field unusable. On the morning of the 15th the big picture became clear. There, not more than ten or twelve miles away, was an enemy transport force offloading men and material. And the Marines could do very little to stop them. They had virtually no fuel and only a few flyable aircraft left. These pitiful air assets were gathered together for a determined effort against the enemy landing.

It is astonishing what can be done with simple determination. Marine mechanics patched together a small number of SBD Dauntless dive bombers and drained fuel from wrecked aircraft which were scattered about, to provide Major General Roy Geiger, the Marine Corps Air Commander, with some kind of attack capability. Even the general's plane, a PBY-5A known as the Blue Goose, was pressed into service. Major Jack Cram, the General's personal pilot, tucked a torpedo under each wing of the lumbering Cat and joined the dive bombers in a sortie against the transports.

The sky over the landing area was alive with fighters but Cram ignored them and, skimming low over the water, aimed the big Cat straight for one of the transports, releasing his fish at close range. One found its mark and ripped a gaping hole in the side of the ship. Then he headed back to Henderson, a swarm of angry Zeros hammering him unmercifully. But there was one thing about Catalinas that others before him had discovered in similar situations. They were tough! The Cat could take an unbelievable amount of abuse and keep flying. Jack Cram and

67

the Blue Goose did just that. As they approached the field, antiaircraft guns on the ground accounted for two of the Zeros. A third followed the Goose down to its final approach and was picked off by an F4F Wildcat.

The Catalina looked like a piece of Swiss cheese as Cram taxied into the line. General Geiger met the plane with a frown on his face and threatened the astonished pilot with a court-martial for the damage done to his aircraft. Then a grin began to appear at the corners of the senior officer's mouth and Cram knew that the general was having his little joke. The major was later awarded the Navy Cross for his audacity.

Five Catalinas operating from the tender *Mackinac* at Vanikoro Island were not so fortunate. On October 14 one of these aircraft, flown by Lieutenant (j.g.) Melvin Butler, made contact with a Japanese task force. He managed to get off a position report and the information that he had been hit. That was all. The plane failed to return to the tender. The remaining four Catalinas were launched at first light the following day to locate the enemy force. They found it. Two of the four PBYs were shot down by heavy antiaircraft fire as the ships zeroed in on the big Cats. Lieutenant (j.g.) Dave Walkinshaw reported the position, course, and speed of two cruisers and three destroyers before beating a successful retreat. One other Cat also escaped destruction.

There were other Cat drivers who also got in on plenty of action during this period. One of them was Lieutenant (j.g.) Alan Rothenberg, who had participated in the night torpedo flight at Midway but had gone home empty-handed. That night had been a big disappointment for him, as well as every man aboard. Now they had a new opportunity.

Rothenberg and his crew had been sent down from Pearl in August to operate in the Solomons as a single-plane detachment from VP-51. They flew many night missions from the tender *Curtiss* at Espiritu Santo. Along with crews from other squadrons, they found the weather to be their worst enemy. Sometimes an entire twelve-hour flight would be flown on instruments, from takeoff to landing. Many hours were spent without making contact with the Japanese, or seeing the water's surface for that matter.

But there were other nights. At about 0200 on October 16, Jim Cobb picked up an enemy formation on radar, descended to a hundred feet, and bore in on it. A few moments later he made visual contact and picked out a large target.

We turned away from the ship and made a couple of practice approaches by radar. They didn't shoot at us. Finally on the fourth approach we got an ideal setup, came in, leading with the radar, and dropped as soon as we could see the ship, which was pretty close. We got a nice hit but we suspect that the torpedo didn't go off. . . . we are afraid we dropped too close to arm.

There was one more torpedo [armed] plane headed for Guadalcanal that night, roughly 180 miles away. We got him on the radio and sent him MOs. He used our MOs and then his radar to come in on. It worked very nicely.[4]

The other plane was 51-P-5 flown by Al Rothenberg. Though a small man in physical stature, in aggressiveness he was as fiesty as they come. Fate had cheated him at Midway, and he would not let *that* happen again.

It had been a long and uneventful flight that night and Cobb's invitation had been especially welcome. As Rothenberg remembers it, the night was dark with not much cloud cover. After picking up a column of ships on radar, he eased the big Cat down to fifty feet. He wanted to make his first run count, and he hoped to give the Japanese as little warning as possible. But restricted vision worked both ways at the lower altitude. Suddenly and unexpectedly a large silhouette loomed directly ahead and Rothenberg horsed back on the yoke to avoid certain collision. He missed hitting an enemy cruiser by only a few feet. It had been a very close call, but there was no time to think about that now. That cruiser was his and he was not going to let it get away. He began a 180-degree turn to port and as he did so suddenly found himself smack in the middle of another darkened column which was steaming parallel to the first. As he banked the Cat sharply overhead, the enemy ships opened up with a hail of antiaircraft fire. Not at all dissuaded by the hostile reception, Rothenberg quickly descended again to fifty feet and headed back toward the first column. Curiously, the enemy fire stopped. Rothenberg had inadvertently placed himself between the two columns so that the frustrated gunners could not shoot at him without endangering their own ships. Now the big silhouette loomed ahead again and this time Rothenberg dropped his fish. As they passed over the column for a second time there was a bright flash of light and a welcome shock wave. The crew of the old Cat knew they had scored.

On the night of October 20 they got another chance to make their presence felt. This time they were armed with 250-pound bombs and had been sent out to find and attack the Tokyo Express. As usual there were no U.S. surface units operating in the area, so that anything they found was fair game. Flying at 1,500 feet they searched for several hours without result. Then as their assigned track carried them off Tassafaronga, they came upon two combatants and two transports. They were close in when the ships were first detected, and Rothenberg nosed the Cat over into a shallow dive. The copilot, Ensign George Coleman held the pickle switch and waited for the plane commander's signal to release the bombs. Rothenberg's plan was to walk his weapons right up to the ship, thus minimizing the chance of dropping long or short. As the target filled the windshield he shouted in quick succession, "Drop one, drop two, drop three, drop four," and Coleman complied. At about this time the enemy vessel opened fire and the air was filled with flying hot metal. The flashes from the gunfire made it impossible to tell whether any of the bombs had hit home. Rothenberg maneuvered violently. To the radioman he barked, "Tell base radio we have attacked a cruiser and the whole Japanese Navy is shooting at us." Then, as a humorous afterthought he added, "And tell them we are returning to base scared stiff."[5] A grinning communications officer met them when they landed and presented Rothenberg with a copy of the message as a souvenir. The conscientious radioman had sent it out just as it had been dictated—word for word.

No one doubted that night combat operations over water were dangerous, but the simple act of taking off or landing at Espiritu Santo after dark was also becoming somewhat hazardous. The island outpost had blossomed overnight into a major supply depot and staging area for military operations in part of the world. Warships, transports, cargo vessels, small craft, and seaplanes seemed to blend together in a collage of activity. One of the memories that is still vivid to George F. "Blackie" Poulos, then a lieutenant with VP-11, is the dark take-offs in a crowded harbor with over 100 ships swinging at anchor.

There were no lights to use as a reference, only the dark silhouettes of the ships so dense that a straight take-off course was not possible. I can still feel the take-offs in the seat of the pants as I snaked the PBY through the ships, feel it get on the step, and then feel the last drop of water drip off as it broke the surface to become airborne.

One morning as I came around a ship, a whaleboat was traversing between two other ships in an obvious collision course from our port side. I concluded that if I could see him he could see and hear me, but such was not the case. When it was obvious we were going to collide, I pulled the port throttle and kicked hard left rudder. In the meantime, the coxswain saw us and turned to his right. He and all his passengers abandoned the whaleboat which went between the PBY's port wing tip float and the port engine's propeller.

I put the port engine back on, straightened my course and continued the take-off and the day's mission. The faithful PBY did not even fall off the step during this drastic maneuver.

On our return from our mission that evening, we learned that the incident was spotted from one of the adjacent ships. All occupants were picked up unharmed and the whaleboat was recaptured after it banged into several ships."[6]

But the PBY pilots were beginning to understand that while night operations were fraught with danger, the darkness also concealed and protected them. And because it covered their approach so well, it injected a new element of surprise into the game and enabled them to exploit natural human apprehensions that come with darkness. They were turning the tables on their nocturnal enemy.

Some of the more innovative Cat crews of VP-11, now operating from the tender *Curtiss* at Espiritu Santo, devised a way to enhance survivability during these night-time forays. Using materials readily at hand they concocted a mixture of soap and lamp black with which they covered the PBYs from nose to tail. The Cats, never known for their great beauty now took on a somewhat shabby and sinister appearance. But on a black night the new look made them almost invisible to surface ships or the occasional floatplane fighter. When encountering the latter, the Cats found that they could descend to skim low over the water so the enemy pilot could not get beneath them. Seen from an overhead position, the black Catalina seemed to blend into the dark surface of the ocean and disappear. If the fighter somehow continued to hold contact and made a diving pass, he risked flying headlong into the sea, for his depth perception was distorted and at that altitude there was no margin for error. It was a very effective defense.

Now the Cats took a page from the Japanese handbook of dirty tricks. One night Jim Cobb took off for Guadalcanal where he would spend several hours giving Japanese troops ashore a taste of their own medicine. Wing racks were loaded with heavy ordnance while inside the aircraft smaller anti-personnel bombs were stashed wherever there was an unoccupied niche. All night they flew back and forth across enemy lines, sometimes making a single drop and sometimes letting their weapons go in a stick of three or four. The bombs which were stowed internally were flipped out of the waist hatch by gleeful crewmen on signal from the pilot. After each pass the PBY would depart the area for a time, suggesting to the enemy that all was clear. Then it would return to repeat the performance. These operations came to be called "Louie the Louse" flights.

That particular night, Cobb may have unwittingly coined the name by

*A VP-12 narrative summary of operations entitled "The Old Black Cats," dated June 29, 1943, credits Commander C. F. Coe, COMAIRSOPAC operations officer, as being the originator of the name "Black Cats." No doubt the term occurred to a number of people independently at one time or another at about the same time, as simply an apt description of this unique aircraft.

which PBYs would become known throughout the South Pacific. As he departed Espiritu Santo for the flight north, he sent word ahead to General Geiger on Guadalcanal that they were coming. In an effort to minimize radio transmissions his short cryptic message read simply, "THE BLACK CAT FLIES TONIGHT."[7]

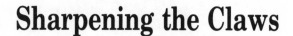

Sharpening the Claws

Vice Admiral John S. McCain was relieved as COMAIRSOPAC on September 20, 1942 by Rear Admiral Aubrey W. Fitch. McCain had done a superb job of organizing and directing land-based air operations for the Guadalcanal campaign and was highly regarded by the Cat crews. "He would ride with us on some of our night missions," remembers Jim Cobb. "It was done without fanfare and he never allowed any publicity. He would just show up before launch time and quietly climb aboard the aircraft."[1] McCain wanted a closer look at Cat operations from the point of view of the men who were actually involved. He needed to know the problems they faced, and what could reasonably be expected from men asked to fly in an unfamiliar nocturnal environment where weather, fatigue, and darkness could kill as suddenly and surely as an antiaircraft barrage. The admiral's unannounced visits had a beneficial effect on crews' morale. Here was a man who was literally willing to put himself in their position. The Cat crews admired him for it and considered McCain one of their own.

Aubrey Fitch, somewhat less personal by nature, was thought by some to be overly aloof. Others swore by him. He was clearly a different personality with a different command philosophy. Fitch made maximum use of the organizational structure and relied heavily on the opinions and recommendations of his staff. He demanded superior performance from his headquarters personnel and he expected them to have the right answers when he needed them. But Fitch was hardly oblivious to the activities of the Cat crews. He too knew that the PBYs turned in the best

Admiral William F. Halsey, Jr. was a colorful and aggressive commander. (U.S. Navy)

results when they operated at night and he intended to develop this concept further. Fitch was known to call individual pilots to his cabin upon their return from night missions to solicit their opinions with regard to the effectiveness of their operations. Al Rothenberg remembers being summoned by Fitch after his night torpedo attack of October 16, and being questioned at some length by the Admiral. Others confirm that this was indeed his practice.

October brought another important change in the organizational structure of the Solomons campaign. On the 18th, overall command of the South Pacific operation passed to Vice Admiral William F. Halsey, Jr. Jim Cobb remembers well that "there was a big change—a tremendous change in the morale of the whole force when Halsey took over from his predecessor. There was a complete turnaround in attitude just from the force of his personality."[2] Indeed Halsey was well known as an aggressive commander, the kind that men will follow anywhere. His prescription for victory was precise and to the point. "Kill Japs, Kill Japs, Kill more Japs!"[3] There was little room for misinterpretation.

Halsey took over as COMSOPAC just in time for one of the major battles of the campaign, in which the Japanese made a concerted effort to annihilate American forces in the area and regain their lost momentum. Their objective ashore was to retake Henderson Field. In addition to the large number of Japanese troops who had been put ashore on the 15th, reinforcements had continued to pour in nightly via the Tokyo Express. Between the 20th and the morning of the 26th, these troops and the ones who were already there made valiant, and in some cases suicidal, attempts to dislodge American ground forces at Henderson, without success. Their casualties numbered in the thousands.

This was a period of considerable activity. Intelligence reported a large build-up of Japanese fleet units at Tonelei Harbor on the southern end of Bougainville. There was little doubt that the enemy was getting ready to send powerful surface forces south to support his ground offensive and to engage any enemy naval units which came forth to fight. But before that happened, the Cats would give them something to think about.

At dusk on October 22, three PBYs of VP-11, with torpedoes tucked under their port wings, took off from Espiritu Santo. Each plane also carried two 500-pound bombs under its starboard wing. It was a 900-mile flight one way and they could not expect to make it all the way back to Espiritu Santo. Instead, they planned to stop at Tulagi to refuel on the way home. This was a flight deep into an enemy-controlled area and there was some question whether they would make it back at all. Lieutenant Jack Coley flew the lead plane, and his navigator and copilot, Joe Deodati, was responsible for the kind of pinpoint navigation on which much of the mission's success depended.

The course ran along the underside of the Solomon chain well out to sea, and the planes made landfall only at Rennell Island and an unnamed reef along the way. Time of arrival at Tonelei Harbor was sometime after 0200 in the early-morning hours of the 23rd. The other two aircraft, flown by Lieutenants Charles F. "Whiskey" Willis and George F. "Blackie" Poulos, kept station on Coley while their navigators tracked him to double-check the progress of the flight. Blackie Poulos remembers the episode distinctly.

It was a bright moonlit night with exceptionally good visibility. In order to avoid detection, we flew the last 150 miles at 20 feet above the water in a tight formation. Jack Coley was the lead plane and his navigation was perfect. We found ourselves going right into the harbor inlet undetected until we had to pull up to avoid hitting the destroyer that was doing sentinel duty at the entrance. Once inside

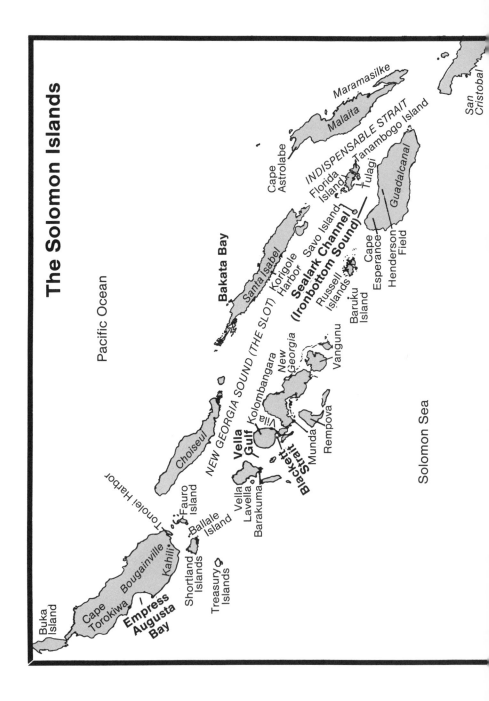

The Solomon Islands

Pacific Ocean

Buka Island

Cape Torokiwa

Bougainville

Kahili

Empress Augusta Bay

Tonolei Harbor

Fauro Island

Ballale Island

Shortland Islands

Treasury Islands

Choiseul

Vella Lavella

Barakuma

Vella Gulf

Kolombangara

Vila

Blackett Strait

Munda

Rempova

New Georgia

Vangunu

NEW GEORGIA SOUND (THE SLOT)

Santa Isabel

Bakata Bay

Korigole Harbor

Savo Island

Sealark Channel (Ironbottom Sound)

Russell Islands

Baruku Island

Florida Island

Tulagi

Tanambogo Island

INDISPENSABLE STRAIT

Cape Astrolabe

Malaita

Maramasilke

Guadalcanal

Cape Esperance

Henderson Field

San Cristobal

Solomon Sea

the harbor the formation split up with each of us seeking his own target. Ships were visible everywhere, mostly destroyers and harbor craft then a larger ship, a heavy cruiser in an uncluttered area—a very good target. I swung to the right to allow enough room to make a good torpedo run, a quick turn to the left with just enough time to stabilize the run, and I pulled the release handle at about 300 yards. During the pull-up to get over the top of the cruiser, I pulled the handle to release two 500-pound bombs. The PBY shuddered as the weapons exploded. The crew members at the waist hatches reported direct hits but it was not possible to determine the extent of the damage. Nevertheless, we knew that we had scored, that we had hurt them, and that they now knew that their sanctuary was not safe from the workhorse PBYs.[4]

Whiskey Willis also remembers hitting Tonelei Harbor on the nose that night. His aircraft, which bore the nickname "Fabulous Character," crossed over a spit of land and burst into the enemy stronghold at fifty feet. It was a breathtaking sight and Willis estimates that there were at least eighty ships there, mostly anchored and silhouetted sharply against the bright moonlight. Surprise was total. The Japanese did not expect American "torpedo planes" to penetrate this far north and certainly not at night.

Willis surveyed the situation quickly and also chose a cruiser as his victim. Lining up on the sleeping giant, he made his run at deck level. As the image of the ship loomed large he dropped his torpedo and pulled up steeply, just missing the superstructure. Seconds later the crew of Fabulous Character was rewarded by a flash and an explosion. Willis now spotted a destroyer also at anchor. It was another sitting duck, but he was coming up on it fast. Making a quick decision, he dropped both his 500-pounders, one on the heels of the other. At least one of these must have hit a magazine for the ship appeared to explode and break in two.

Joe Deodati in Coley's plane recalls that they had really come looking for carriers, but found none. "Instead," he says, "we slammed a torpedo into an armed transport ship. We also attacked an unknown combatant ship with skip bombs with questionable success."[5] Now all hell broke loose. "It was like the fourth of July," said Willis. "We stayed right on the deck as we made our escape and the Japanese had to depress their guns to shoot at us. I'm sure they must have hit each other with all that stuff flying around."[6]

All three planes made it out of the harbor and headed for Tulagi independently. Coley's aircraft had taken several hits and as a result had lost all fuel from the starboard wing tank. This was serious because even under normal conditions there was not that much fuel to spare. Coley throttled back and carefully leaned the engines to get as many miles as possible out of the remaining fuel. Miraculously, they made it all the way to land at Tulagi that morning with a few gallons left over. The other two Cats also arrived safely at Tulagi, and the subsequent flight back to Espirito Santo was uneventful.

As part of their new push against Guadalcanal, the Japanese threw a large naval force into the area which included four carriers, four battleships, and a number of cruisers, destroyers, and other vessels. The Americans had but two carriers, the *Enterprise* and *Hornet*, plus two battleships, nine cruisers, and some twenty-four destroyers. The engagement which resulted is now known as the Battle of the Santa Cruz Islands.

At first the two forces jockeyed for position, neither making contact

Three Cats head north at dusk. (U.S. Navy)

with the other. Then on the 23rd one of the Cats located a Japanese carrier and the pace quickened. After dark Fitch launched several torpedo-armed PBYs to find and sink it. But the elusive aircraft carrier seemed to have vanished. Only Lieutenant (j.g.) George Enloe of VP-11 and his crew turned up hard evidence that the Japanese were operating in the area. What they found was a heavy cruiser and although it was not what they were looking for, it was better than nothing. Enloe made a low approach and released his fish before the Japanese knew they were under attack. But there was no explosive flash telling the Cat crew they had scored. Having expended their only shot, they headed for home.

Subsequently the area lapsed into the eerie silence that often seems to precede a battle. Then on the 25th a PBY-5A from VP-24 flown by Lieutenant (j.g.) "Doc" Mathews discovered a powerful Japanese task force which included the battleship *Haruna*. This was a daylight search mission and the aircraft had no torpedoes aboard with which to attack. But the opportunity was too good to pass up. Having reported his find to base radio, Mathews made a single run at the *Haruna* and dropped the only weapons he had—two 500-pound flat-nosed depth charges, which he released from a considerable distance. Then he wrapped the airplane into a tight turn to high-tail it out of the area. What happened to the depth charges is not known but the *Haruna* ignored the insult and steamed on. Three floatplanes pounced on the Cat before she could get clear. First radioman Ewing W. "Bill" Hix, who was then manning the starboard gun, took careful aim and squeezed the trigger as they made their runs on the big Cat. Plane Captain Elmer Parker straddled the center line between the two blisters and coolly reloaded the empty 50-round cannisters as the cartridges were expended. Hix, who had been with Dagwood Probst at Midway, remembered with satisfaction that he "burned one and damaged another."[7] After that, the floatplanes broke off and the PBY returned to base without further incident.

Other elements of the Japanese fleet were also discovered that day by PBYs and B-17s, and when darkness came five more Cats loaded with bombs and torpedoes took off to try their luck. At about 0250 on the morning of the 26th, the carrier *Zuikaku* almost became a casualty when a Catalina suddenly dove out of the blackness to deliver a stick of four bombs which barely missed its intended victim. The destroyer *Isokaze* was similarly assaulted but also escaped damage.

At 0500 the *Enterprise* launched sixteen Dauntless dive bombers to join the search, and at 0512 the task force commanders received word of another PBY contact which had occurred about two hours earlier. Back at his headquarters in Nouméa, New Caledonia, Admiral Halsey read the message traffic and decided that the time was ripe for action. A terse

79

A native chief at the Stewart Islands paddles out to parley with the pilot of a VP-91 Cat which has just landed in the lagoon. (Captain D. Walkinshaw collection)

message was transmitted to the fleet that was pure Halsey: "ATTACK— REPEAT—ATTACK."[8]

In the carrier duel which followed, two of the enemy flattops were put out of action. On the other side of the ledger, the *Hornet* was severely damaged and could not be saved. By the end of the day on the 26th, the battle of the carriers and their aircraft was over. But in the wee hours of the morning on the 27th, the PBYs were getting in their last licks.

At about 0200 one of the Cats from Espiritu Santo attempted another attack on the carrier *Zuikaku*, this time with a torpedo, but did not score. A second Cat from VP-91 had better fortune and helped to even the score for the three aircraft lost by that squadron less than two weeks before. Lieutenant (j.g.) Melvin K. Atwell and his crew came upon the destroyer

Teruzuki at about 0100 and began a glide-bombing run. Two 500-pound bombs were slung under each wing and Atwell elected to employ them in groups of two, one pair following seconds behind the other. They would use the manual-release handles, one of which was located on each side of the cockpit controlling the weapons load on that side of the aircraft. Atwell had instructed his copilot not to release the bombs under the starboard wing until he had dropped those on the port side. As the Cat dove on the target, Atwell readied his drop by taking up the slack in his release handle. The copilot, thinking Atwell had dropped the port-side bombs, released his bombs just before Atwell actually pulled his handle. The copilot's bombs hit about seventy-five feet astern while Atwell's two 500-pounders struck the ship just aft of the stacks. Altitude was well under six hundred feet when the weapons exploded. Shrapnel ripped through the hull of the aircraft. The impact blew away the radio antenna, broke radio tubes, and extinguished all lights. The Cat was tossed about like a tennis ball as Atwell struggled to maintain control. When they finally returned to base the plane was full of holes and one wing was

Beached Japanese ship rests on the bottom at Ironbottom Sound off Guadalcanal. (Captain G. Bogart collection)

found to be badly warped. But it was all worth it. The *Teruzuki* limped home but would be out of the game for awhile.

So ended the Battle of the Santa Cruz Islands. It was another victory of sorts for the Japanese. The *Hornet* was lost and surface units, including the battleship *South Dakota*, sustained significant damage. Still, the Japanese carriers *Zuiho* and *Shokaku* had also been hurt, the *Shokaku* severely. So were the cruiser *Chikuma* and the destroyer *Teruzuki*. Most important, the enemy had failed in his dual objective of retaking Henderson Field and driving the U.S. Navy from the Solomons. The days of Japanese supremacy at sea were rapidly drawing to a close.

It was a time of uneasiness for the enemy. The Americans seemed to have halted the hitherto steady advance of Imperial Japan. New and more powerful combatant ships were now joining the U.S. fleet. While still quantitatively inferior, the U.S. Navy in the South Pacific was growing almost daily in size, experience, and confidence.

The naval Battle of Guadalcanal was fought in mid-November. It was an engagement of surface ships, carrier planes, and land-based aircraft from Henderson Field. Losses were heavy on both sides. The enemy succeeded in putting about 2,000 troops and some supplies ashore on Guadalcanal, but lost eleven transports in the process. Two Japanese battleships were also sunk and a large number of aircraft destroyed.

On the last day of that same month it was the Americans who came off on the bitter end, at the Battle of Tassafaronga. The cruiser *Northampton* was sunk in this night engagement and severe damage was inflicted on three other U.S. cruisers. The Japanese fought superbly and lost only one destroyer in that fight. But despite the outcome, the enemy now knew that he could not venture south in force, even at night, and expect to be unopposed.

The Japanese were faced with a dilemma. They had not given up on the idea of retaking Guadalcanal, and their troops there still required logistics support which could only come from the sea. To accomplish this task, fast destroyers were sent to run into Ironbottom Sound* at night and drop buoyant drums into the sea close to the beach, where they could be picked up by small boats. The destroyers no longer dared to linger while cargoes were offloaded in a more conventional manner. Submarines and barges were also employed. These measures were far from being satisfactory solutions to a difficult problem, but they did enable the enemy to continue a flow of supplies, albeit greatly reduced, to their forces ashore.

By this time, the Japanese had decided that if they were ever going to

*Ironbottom Sound was the name given to the body of water between Guadalcanal and Florida Island (otherwise known as Sealark Channel) because so many ships of both sides were sunk there during the Solomons campaign.

82

Black Cat base. Jet-black aircraft contrast with white sand. (U.S. Navy)

dislodge the Americans on Guadalcanal they would need land-based air to cover their supply and reinforcement operations. They would also need land-based fighter escort for bomber attacks on American positions ashore as well as the sea-based supply line. Consequently, on November 24 they began construction of an airfield at Munda Point on New Georgia Island, about 150 miles northwest of Guadalcanal. Logistics support for this venture was provided at night by the "Tokyo Express."

With all their other mounting troubles, the Japanese operating forces were now becoming aware of still another unpleasant development. Something was out there lurking in the night sky—something with eyes that pierced the darkness but could not be seen—something that lay in wait for Japanese warships and cargo vessels and struck without warning. It was a new and discomforting experience and they did not know exactly how to deal with it.

Cats Are Night Creatures

It was necessity which obliged the Japanese to supply their positions and outposts ashore almost exclusively at night. Their ships and barges moved mostly in small convoys guarded by one or more combatant vessels. These operations were carried on throughout the area and it was virtually impossible for U.S. surface combatant forces to stop them.

Ironically, it was also necessity which had turned the PBYs into night creatures. Their slow speeds, which rendered them clumsy and vulnerable by day, made them agile and surefooted by night. Radio altimeters allowed them to skim the dark surface of the ocean where fast fighters feared to tread. Their size, which made them easy daylight targets, enabled them to carry large quantities of fuel and weapons, and to range deep into enemy-controlled areas after dark. They could remain aloft all night, searching out their prey with electronic eyes or lying in wait at strategic points. The Black Cat concept developed naturally through the survival instinct and the determination to strike back against a cruel and unrelenting enemy. No one man or group can be given credit for its genesis. It was the result of the contributions and sacrifices of many, a combination of courage, technology, and the hard lessons of combat.

Aubrey Fitch was now ready to use this capability aggressively against the "Tokyo Express." He had already decided to officially designate one unit a Black Cat squadron and deploy it to a forward area to evaluate the idea. Its planes would take off at dusk and return home at first light. All aircraft in the squadron would be equipped with radar and radio altimeters, and painted with non-reflective black paint. Even the aircraft side numbers would be obliterated so as not to provide a focal point for enemy searchlights.

The squadron chosen for the initial honor was VP-12. Its skipper, Commander Clarence Orville Taff, was somewhat more senior than other patrol squadron COs and Fitch knew that he could count on his experience and mature judgment to make this venture a success. Soft-spoken but firm of purpose, Taff was an ideal man for the job. His Executive Officer Lieutenant Ronald R. Stultz remembers him as "a wise and natural leader," who "was extremely well liked by all in his squadron and was respected by the Air Staffs at Guadalcanal and AIRSOPAC."[1] One VP-12 pilot, Lieutenant (j.g.) Moreno Caparrelli later wrote of Taff that he "planned our missions, briefed us, straightened out our troubles and flew on all the hardest tasks."[2]

The squadron was at Nandi Air Base in the Fiji Islands, conducting routine and uneventful patrols, when word came that they would be moving up to the Solomons, where the action was. At daybreak on December 10, Lieutenant Stultz took off for New Caledonia with the first three planes. There they would be fitted with radio altimeters and painted flat black. The flight encountered a lot of rain along the way, but this was routine during the winter months in this part of the world. In all, the flight to New Caledonia was uneventful and they arrived on sched-ule. Then on the 11th Stultz had a landing mishap and his plane sank to the wings. It had to be shipped off the island for major repairs. The accident was a great disappointment for Stultz and his crew, because it meant an uncertain period of delay in getting to the forward area.

The other two planes flown by Lieutenants William Pack and Ray Tylutki got their black paint and radio altimeters according to plan and proceeded on to Espiritu Santo. There fate dealt them another blow. A Flying Fortress went out of control on landing, careened across the field and smashed into Pack's parked PBY. Radioman Henry Ledoux took the accident personally and vented his frustration in his diary. "Some God damned B-17 plowed right into our ship," he wrote with obvious irrita-tion. "I can't express how bad it made us feel and, as for Lieutenant Pack, he was speechless."[3] In all, it was an inauspicious beginning for the first Black Cat squadron.

Ray Tylutki and his crew proceeded on alone, arriving at Henderson Field on the 15th. The following day they were put to work. Another B-17 had gone down at the southern tip of Tetipari Island, some 35 miles south of the new Japanese airfield at Munda Point on New Georgia Island. Tylutki was dispatched to attempt a rescue, with four Grumman Wildcat fighters for cover. He set the Cat down in the open sea and taxied in close to the beach. There he remained for almost forty minutes while the ten

85

crewmen slowly made their way to the big seaplane. Six men swam and four others paddled in a rubber boat. All were happy to be pulled safely aboard. The copilot, Warrant Officer William W. Gardner, made the takeoff in heavy swells. The plane bounced five times before it gained enough speed for Gardner to horse it off the water. But the seams held and the Cat returned to base.

That same night, Tylutki was sent out again, this time on a harassing attack on Munda airfield. He carried four 500-pound bombs under the wings and a number of smaller fragmentation bombs which were stowed inside the aircraft on the bunks. He spent the night in the Munda area, flying over the airfield at irregular intervals to drop a 500-pounder or some frags. It is questionable how much damage they may have done, but the Japanese were certainly kept from sleeping very much and their productiveness must have been decreased the following day.

Ron Stultz had in the meantime received a replacement aircraft, modified it for Black Cat operations, and arrived at Guadalcanal a few days later. The first job at hand was to set up a suitable place for the squadron to live and work. They found that there were no ideal locations at Henderson and the area assigned was typical of the other encampments—a quagmire of reeking black mud. There they set up tents over steel Marston matting, a material designed for the temporary fabrication of runways and aircraft parking aprons. The tents provided reasonable shelter from the frequent rain showers, but the mud oozed up through the perforations in the Marston matting when it was stepped upon, and sometimes the matting disappeared completely from sight and was never seen again.

This was, of course, mosquito country and there was little relief from the siege of these bloodthirsty insects. Squadron personnel swore that the beasts were radar-equipped. In addition to producing extreme discomfort, the mosquitoes brought with them the danger of malaria and other tropical diseases which threatened the health and operational efficiency of the squadron. But there was no help for it. This was the way men lived on Guadalcanal.

Lieutenant Pack and his replacement aircraft arrived at Henderson Field on Christmas Day. With him was an officer from Fitch's staff who had come along to brief two crews on a night torpedo-attack mission planned for that night. Among the VP-12 aircraft commanders who had arrived thus far, only Stultz had any experience with torpedo drops. Consequently, he went along as copilot on Lieutenant Norm Pedersen's aircraft to assist in launching the weapons. The staff officer flew copilot for Pack and his crew. The plan was to fly to Bougainville Island, about 300 miles to the north, where they expected to find a number of Japanese

VP-12 Squadron CO, Commander Clarence Orville Taff and mascot "Yardbird." (Mrs. Warren S. Pittman collection)

ships at anchor. Because the enemy controlled this area, it was hoped that the attack would be a surprise and that maximum damage might be inflicted.

The two planes took off at dusk, each carrying two torpedoes set to run for 600 yards before becoming armed. Maintaining radio silence from the start, the two aircraft soon became separated in the darkness, attesting to the effectiveness of their black camouflage. As a result they each

87

PBY
CATALINA

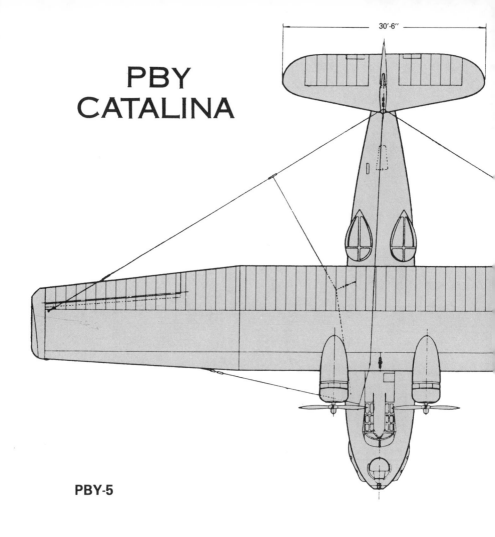

30'-6"

PBY-5

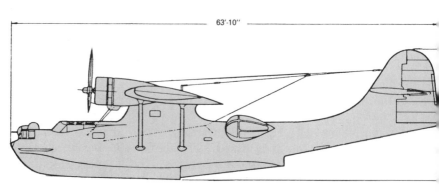

63'-10"

88

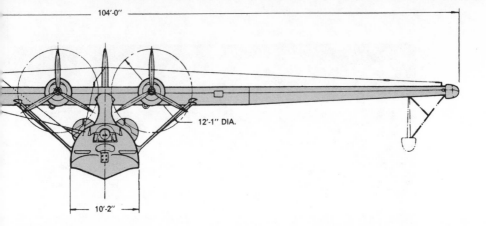

104'-0"

12'-1" DIA.

10'-2"

PBY-5

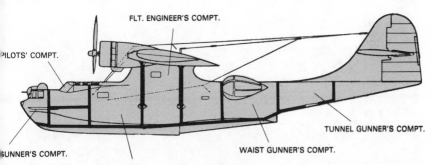

FLT. ENGINEER'S COMPT.

PILOTS' COMPT.

TUNNEL GUNNER'S COMPT.

WAIST GUNNER'S COMPT.

GUNNER'S COMPT.

NAVIGATOR/RADIOMAN/RADARMAN'S COMPT.

PBY CATALINA

	PBY-5	PBY-5A
Wing span	104 ft.	104 ft.
Length	63 ft. 10 in.	63 ft. 10 in.
Height	18 ft. 10 in.	20 ft. 2 in.
Wing area	14000 sq. ft.	14000 sq. ft.
Gross weight	31800 lbs.	34000 lbs.
Engine (2)	R-1830	R-1830
Horsepower (T.O.)	1200	1200
Max. speed (7000 ft.)	195 mph	180 mph
Cruising speed	110 mph	117 mph
Service ceiling	18000 ft.	15000 ft.
Range	2850 mi.	2550 mi.

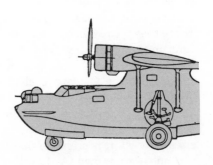

PBY-5A

89

Performance data approx.

Officer's barber shop, Guadalcanal. Black Cat pilots gave each other haircuts. (Mrs. Warren S. Pittman collection)

proceeded independently toward the target area. Pedersen and Stultz continued on course until just short of the southern tip of Bougainville. There they picked up a small island on radar and made practice torpedo runs on it as they went by.

A crescent moon hung low in the sky, silhouetting objects on the surface. As the Cat approached the outer harbor a low lying shape became visible. Pedersen made a 360-degree turn while Stultz set up for an attack. All was ready as they rolled out of the turn and the big plane eased down closer to the water. There was no indication of alarm on the enemy vessel. It is probable that they had heard the Cat but assumed it was one of their own. At 1,000 yards Stultz released his fish. Pedersen pulled up and flew directly over the target, at which time Stultz dropped a flare. The PBY crew was surprised to discover that they had attacked an

I-class submarine. Even more startled were the Japanese sitting on deck in the warm tropical night. Stultz recalls that the after lookouts reported no flash or anything that would indicate a hit, "so that we again reversed and came back over the area. On the surface of the water was debris and a considerably riled-up foamed area. Not wishing to make our presence known any more than necessary we continued on into the inner harbor where many shapes were visible to the eye."

The Cat chose another target, lined up, and began its run. Again the torpedo was released at the appropriate distance and again Stultz dropped a flare "almost to my lasting regret for the ship turned out to be a destroyer which immediately opened fire with machine-gun and antiaircraft bursts. The antiaircraft bursts were ineffective as we were at masthead height and directly over their ship. The small-caliber fire, however, was quite heavy and straddled us as they picked us up with searchlights."[5] Unfortunately, either the Cat's aim was off or the torpedo had not run true. The destroyer turned sharply and moved away at high speed. "We did not linger in the harbor once our torpedoes were expended but headed back to Henderson Field where we soon heard of the exciting flight of Lieutenant Pack and his crew."[6]

Pack arrived in the target area shortly after Pedersen and Stultz had departed. They spent some time selecting a suitable target and finally came upon four destroyers anchored off Fauro Island in Bougainville Strait. This was what they were after and the staff officer who was flying copilot began a low turn toward the enemy ships while Pack checked to see that all was in readiness for the drop. Then as they continued to close the target in a circling approach, the copilot apparently misjudged his altitude and the plane edged dangerously close to the water's surface. Pack grabbed for the yoke but he was too late. The aircraft hit the water in a skid and the impact tore a huge hole "the size of a bathtub" in the port side of the hull.[7] By this time the destroyers had spotted the would-be attacker and had begun to fire on the wounded Cat with everything they had. Pack jammed the throttles full forward and fought to keep the plane moving. The sea poured in through the opening as the engines strained to lift two torpedoes and an undetermined amount of water. Miraculously the Cat staggered back into the air and hung there with the enemy destroyers now firing furiously at point-blank range. Perhaps it was the proximity of 200 to 600 yards that confounded the enemy gunners and gave the Catalina a fighting chance.

Pack jettisoned the two torpedoes to lighten the aircraft and quickly moved out of range into the blackness. Sometime later they made it back to Henderson Field. There they discovered that the nose wheel had been damaged by the unscheduled water landing and would not extend. Pack brought the plane down as gingerly as possible and held the nose off as long as he could. Then as they lost speed, the nose made contact with the ground and the aircraft skidded to a grinding halt. The experience brought home the hazards of low-altitude night attacks over water. It reminded all involved that the ultimate penalty for a slight miscalculation lurked only a few feet below in the cruel and unforgiving sea.

And so Christmas came and went without much outward recognition. Although many found time to pause and reflect on personal commitments to a larger order of things, most just thought about home and wished they were there.

If Christmas had been less festive than desired, Norm Pedersen had something in mind to usher in the new year. He and his crew were scheduled to fly a night harassment mission against Munda airfield on December 31, and in preparation they began hoarding empty beer bottles. Someone claimed that they made an eerie whistling sound when dropped from altitude and would be just the thing for a "Louie the louse" flight.

On New Year's Eve they took off and headed for Munda, arriving in the area after dark. By midnight they had expended three of their four 500-pound bombs and all of their frags. But Pedersen had carefully saved one of the heavies for just the right moment. Timing his last run carefully he watched the sweep second hand of the eight-day clock on the instrument panel approach twelve. As it passed the other two hands he blew the warning horn, dropped the remaining 500-pound bomb and launched a flare at the same time. The crew responded by throwing all their beer bottles overboard. "Happy New Year!" they all shouted.[8] A few minutes later the relief aircraft flown by Pappy Kennon and crew arrived on station. Pedersen and company headed home with the boast that they had been the first to bomb the Japanese in 1943.

Flight operations in the new year continued without let-up. On the night of January 4, two Black Cats flown by Lieutenants Hadley Lewis and Norm Pedersen were assigned to spot for the bombardment of Munda by the light cruisers *Nashville, St. Louis,* and *Helena,* and destroyers *Fletcher* and *O'Bannon.* That evening they departed Henderson Field and conducted a search for enemy surface forces to a distance of 100 miles northwest of the target. Finding no sign of Japanese warships which might oppose the operation, they returned to Munda and took station 10,000 feet overhead.

They did not have to wait long for the action to start. The surface vessels had already arrived and were making final preparations for the bombardment. Suddenly sometime after 0100 it began, with a salvo which landed squarely on the airfield. Fire-control spotters aboard the

92

A Black Cat navigator reports the aircraft's progress to the plane commander. (Mrs. Warren S. Pittman collection)

two Cats were in radio contact with the warships and began feeding them information, walking the big projectiles back and forth across the enemy positions. The Cat crews had never seen anything like it. It seemed like a steady sheet of flame from ship to shore and it lasted for fully twenty minutes. It was the Henderson Field bombardment all over again, but this time the Japanese were on the receiving end.

From the beginning, VP-12 operated from Henderson Field in split shifts. Half the planes and crews were at Guadalcanal for three of four weeks while the rest of the squadron flew their missions from Espiritu Santo. Then they traded off. It was a good arrangement because living conditions in the forward area were very primitive. Malaria and other tropical diseases ran rampant and were carried freely by the swarms of vicious mosquitoes whose larvae flourished in the oozing black mud, the pools of putrid green water, and the incessant jungle heat. These problems added significantly to the perils inherent in low-level night operations. Flight-crew members often flew with fever, chills, diarrhea, and other ailments simply because it was their turn to go and there was no one else. Ronald Stultz, VP-12 Executive Officer remembers the problem well. "Our squadron was infected with malaria quite heavily, 85% might be a good figure. Although atabrine tablets were taken daily, the toll was still quite high. Many found that small scratches became sores that ulcerated and took weeks to cure. Antibiotics were not known, nor penicillin at that time. The sulpha-drugs were available and the sulpha powders were our friends for these sores. Some squadron members, however, did not even respond to this treatment and ultimately required evacuation and hospitalization for the 'jungle rot.' "[9] By the end of February, Radioman Ledoux recorded in his diary that, "Malaria has just about knocked out most of the squadron. Most flight crews are composed of odds and ends. In our crew only Ragusa and I are left out of the original crew. McKinney, our Chief A.P. [enlisted pilot] is still here too."[10]

As a matter of routine, each crew flew a mission every third night and sometimes more frequently. Because of the special capabilities of the Catalina, they were often called out during the day as well for special rescue missions, mostly involving downed pilots and crewmen.

At night, "Washing Machine Charlie" arrived over Henderson at un-

A popular chore—emptying beer bottles to drop on the Japanese. (U.S. Navy)

94

predictable hours, dropping occasional bombs that kept maintenance personnel and off-duty flight crews from getting much sleep. Muddy foxholes, sometimes half-filled with water, offered little sleeping comfort. While fight-crew members were often able to catch catnaps after the sun rose, morning found the maintenance people back on the job, working through the blistering heat of the day to keep the Cats airborne at night. They did their jobs well.

And if there were not enough other hazards, the Black Cat crewmen of VP-12 often created their own. Radioman First Class Henry Ledoux, a member of Lieutenant Pack's crew, was always looking for action. His idea of relaxation during off-duty hours was to gather together a few like-minded friends and hitch a ride to the front lines on Guadalcanal. There they could exchange war stories with the Marines and perhaps get off a few shots at the Japanese themselves. The Black Cat crewmen seemed to enjoy observing the war from a different perspective, and on one occasion Ledoux went into a hot area under fire and helped carry out a wounded infantryman.

The Marines were quite hospitable to the plucky Ledoux and his friends. If they wanted to get their heads blown off it was no skin off their noses. In one trip to the front, Ledoux reported, "We were on the top of a long ridge and on each side of us was a deep valley. Jap snipers were not over 150 yards away, just popping away. Every now and then one would come pretty close and you could hear the 'zing' and duck down in the fox-hole for a while."[11] It was good sport!

Other members of the squadron went for somewhat milder diversions. Aviation Machinist's Mate First Class Eddie Siebler of Lieutenant Roger Wolfe's crew was known as one of the best rat catchers in the outfit. He used an overturned ammunition box propped up with a stick attached to a long string. When a big rat ventured under the box for a tasty morsel, Siebler pulled the string and captured his prey. There were plenty of rats to go around and several crewmen participated in this sport. Chess was a popular game among the deep thinkers. Others captured some of the small red parrots which abounded on the island and tried to teach them to talk. If any of these birds picked up extensive vocabularies one can only hope that they did not pass any of the words on to their offspring after the Americans left.

Considering the harsh conditions at Henderson, morale was superb. The members of the first official Black Cat squadron were a hearty lot and took great pride in their accomplishments. With characteristic good humor they developed a system by which one could tell at a glance the prowess of a crew or something of the combat experience of an individual. After one bombing mission a basic cat could be painted on an aircraft or

95

on the back of a shirt or a flight jacket.* After two such missions, eyes could be added. Three qualified a crew for teeth and whiskers. But the real prize involved the greatest risk, a night torpedo attack. After one of these, the cat could be adorned with anatomical accessories of a more personal nature.

The squadron also boasted a mascot, a genuine coal-black feline of indeterminate lineage. Someone had picked up the cat in the Fijis and brought it along to Guadalcanal. "Yardbird," as the cat was called, led a good life, with scraps from the mess tent and all the fat rats she could catch. Some claimed that the rats were larger than Yardbird, but whatever the case, the cat seemed well able to hold its own. Yardbird got plenty of attention from the flight crews and frequently went along on night missions. And it was said that, true to the old superstition the black cat did bring bad luck—in this case to the Japanese.**

Commander Taff arrived on Guadalcanal during the second week of January to relieve Lieutenant Stultz and his contingent. There was barely time to get settled, for Taff was anxious to go out after the Tokyo Express, which was still making regular supply runs to Japanese troops on Guadalcanal and other islands in the Solomons.

Early on the Cats had instituted the "Mike Search" designed to catch the elusive Japanese as they made their way south down the Slot or tried an end run by way of Indispensable Strait. The search pattern began at Savo Island and then proceeded almost due west to Buraku Island, about halfway between the Russells and Vangunu of the New Georgia Group. From there it struck north, across the Slot to Korigole Harbor located midway down the southwestern coast of Santa Isabel Island, then southeast along the edge of that land mass and across Indispensable Strait to Cape Astrolabe on the northernmost tip of Malaita. Thence back to Savo. The entire circuit required three of more hours to complete, depending upon what one found along the way. Three circuits were the usual fare for one night mission, and total elapsed time ran eleven hours on the average. Weather in the area was usually bad and the pilots found themselves making trade-offs between the best radar-search altitude of about 1,500–2,000 feet and a much lower altitude to sneak under clouds and avoid running headlong into a thunderhead. Some of the islands in the area had volcanic peaks; these were a hazard in themselves to a Cat flying under instrument conditions at low altitude with an inoperative radar set. Yet the "Mike Search" was considered a must and was rarely can-

*Despite the searing heat of the day, leather flight jackets were usually worn at altitude (10,000 feet or more) during night gunfire-spotting missions.

**When VP-12 returned to the U.S., Aviation Ordnanceman Eugene L. Davies took the cat back to California with him.

A game of foxhole chess. (VP-12 cruise book)

celled. It was deemed essential that enemy surface activity be choked off.

On January 14 Taff led three Cats out among the islands to seek out the Japanese ships. If they were there, he was determined to find them. The pilots of the other two aircraft, Lieutenants Cyrenus L. Gillette and Hadley Lewis, were no less resolved.

It was a black night and the weather, as usual, made visual contact difficult. In fact, it was hard for the three planes to maintain their loose formation. After several hours of searching without finding a sign of the enemy, one of the Cats picked up a radar contact at six miles. Taff's PBY, nicknamed "Heartless Henry," turned toward the target, the other two aircraft following at prudent intervals. The wakes of the enemy ships were first to come into view. Several destroyers, it was difficult to tell how many, were headed for Guadalcanal. The three planes moved in quickly and made their drops. Because of the darkness and the bad weather no one knows for certain whether any solid hits were made, but when it was all over the destroyers were seen to have turned tail and fled.

Two nights later, Taff and Gillette in one PBY and Lieutenant Stanley Stanul in another conducted a night bombing raid on Kihili airfield on Bougainville, dropping a total of eight 500-pounders and a number of 20-pound anti-personnel bombs. It is impossible to say how much havoc was created, but at least one large fire was started on the airfield. To the

97

Crew members load chow aboard a Black Cat before a mission. (VP-12 cruise book)

Japanese on the ground, the sound of enemy aircraft overhead was a relatively new experience and they must have wondered about its portent for the future.

A few miles to the northwest of Munda and across the Kula Gulf lay volcanic Kolombangara Island with peaks of over 5,500 feet. On the flat area along the shore at Vila Plantation, the enemy was busily constructing another airfield which could support strikes against Guadalcanal and U.S. fleet units. They were also using this site as a transshipment point for supplies bound for Munda. Encouraged by the success of the Munda bombardment of January 4–5, Admiral Halsey decided to have a go at Vila. The *Nashville* and *Helena* would do the honors with their 6-inch guns on the night of January 23–24, and the destroyers *Nicholas*, *DeHaven*, *Radford*, and *O'Bannon* would chime in with their 5-inch mounts. Taff and Gillette conducted the spotting operation.

It was essentially a repeat of the previous operation at Munda with the spotters calling the plays to saturate the enemy airfield. The Japanese launched a flight of Bettys to attack the surface force but these were driven off by antiaircraft fire. The black PBYs circling overhead were never engaged and their presence may not even have been suspected by the enemy. The shelling, on the other hand, was a complete success. Both Vila and Munda would get much more attention of this sort.

The weather was not always cooperative on these missions, as was illustrated by the experience of Lieutenant Roger Wolfe on the night of

January 26. Wolfe and his crew had returned to base from a night mission against Munda at about 0115, only to find the field socked in. Henderson control advised him to orbit in the clear until conditions improved. Wolfe complied, but the bad weather persisted. Just before dawn, with only ten to fifteen minutes of fuel remaining, Wolfe decided to land in the open sea while he still had power, rather than be forced to risk a dead-stick attempt in the dark. Dropping smoke lights for visual reference he made his approach into the wind. As he touched down, the nose dipped into a heavy swell. The momentum drove the plane under and it immediately filled with water. Crewmen exited the stricken Cat as best they could and congregated on the wing which was still afloat. When all heads were counted, Ensign Gordon Gustafson the navigator had not made it out. By then more than ten minutes had gone by, and it was feared that he had drowned. Just then his head popped to the surface and he was dragged sputtering and coughing onto the wing. He had been knocked senseless by the impact and came to in an air bubble at the top of the aircraft. Groping around in the darkness underwater he finally made it out through one of the blisters.

But they were all far from safe. The wing kept the airplane from sinking for the time being but it too would eventually go down. Wolfe dove down into the fuselage and, after several tries managed to retrieve two rafts from the plane. They inflated these, climbed aboard, and abandoned the doomed Cat. When daylight came they found themselves adrift in the open sea with no land in sight. But they had a good idea of their position and some thirty-six hours later were able to make the island of Buraku. They had neither food nor water but were able to eke out meager sustenance from raw fish and coconuts for another two and a half days. Then they were spotted by two Army P-40s, and later rescued by a PBY.

Weather was perhaps the greatest hazard faced by the Black Cat crews. Aircraft often took off on instruments and flew an entire patrol without visual contact with the surface. One night in early February, three Cats took off in a blinding rain to search for a large Japanese task force spotted north of Rabaul and heading south at eighteen knots. One Cat ran into a front only sixty miles north of Henderson. Mauled by violent drafts and unable to find a hole through the front, he finally returned to base. Another Cat was able to complete about half of the assigned course, seeing little along the way. A third aircraft had flown the entire circuit in heavy rain, not once making visual contact with anything until landing at Henderson the next morning. At one point in the flight the navigator dryly asked the pilot, Lieutenant Hartsel "Red" Allen, if they were still taxiing and if so, when did he expect to get airborne?

Commander Aircraft, South Pacific Force
Pacific Fleet

April 10, 1943.

From: Commander Aircraft, South
             Pacific Force.
To: Commander, Patrol Squadron
             Twelve.

Subject: Original Black Cat Squadron.

1.   This is to certify for the edi-
fication of posterity that the squadron which
initially developed and conducted the highly
effective night tactics peculiar to "Black
Cats" is Patrol Squadron Twelve. The name
"Black Cat" was originated by this command
about December 14, 1942, as a term descrip-
tive of the aircraft of Patrol Squadron Twelve
which were specially prepared for these operations.

2.   While many other squadrons will
follow in the footsteps of Patrol Squadron
Twelve and be known as "Black Cats", the
honor of being the original Black Cat Squadron definitely belongs to Patrol Squadron
Twelve.

AUBREY W. FITCH.

VP-12 was the Navy's first official Black Cat squadron. (VP-12 cruise book)

On the night of February 1–2 the Japanese made their move to evacuate Guadalcanal. About twenty enemy destroyers made a high-speed run
down the Slot under cover of aircraft for most of the way. American dive
bombers and torpedo planes attacked the force and damaged one destroyer off the southeastern end of the New Georgia group of islands.
After dark, PT boats made a brave attempt to stop the Japanese task

100

force as they moved closer to Guadalcanal, but to no avail. One enemy destroyer hit a mine and was lost but the others picked up their cargoes of half-starved and demoralized troops and headed north.

They tried it again two days later and again they were met by U.S. dive bombers and attack planes which disabled one ship but only slightly damaged a few others. That night a Black Cat dropped flares on the enemy task force so Dauntless dive bombers could make their attacks. But there were no hits. The Japanese were again successful.

On the night of February 7–8 the last evacuation run took place, and on the 9th American ground forces were able to report that the enemy had pulled up stakes completely and was gone. The Japanese had lost about 25,000 men on Guadalcanal. They had also lost their forward momentum and, much worse, they had allowed the Americans to reverse its direction. The movement of the fighting was now proceeding to the northwest, up the Solomons chain toward their major stronghold—Rabaul!

But the work of the Black Cats was only beginning. The Japanese would now have to supply and support their new bases at Vila and Munda and several other key points among the islands by night. The Catalinas continued to disrupt these logistics runs. And they also carried out bombing and harassment missions, rescue flights, and spotting for surface gunfire as well.

By March 27, VP-12 had flown 236 missions, mostly at night, for a total of 1,660 hours. These included bombing, torpedo, gunfire spotting, search, convoy, antisubmarine, and rescue operations. Officers and men received personal decorations for their performance, and the squadron as a whole was awarded a Presidential Unit Citation as "The first Catalina squadron to operate from Guadalcanal and the originator of the highly effective night tactics peculiar to 'Black Cats'. . . . Outstanding for its indomitable fighting spirit, Patrol Squadron Twelve established a standard for subsequent Catalina squadrons and achieved a gallant record of service which reflects the highest credit upon its pilots and crews and the United States Naval Service."[12]

It was a good beginning.

Drink to the Black Cat

So drink to the Black Cat PBY
Damnedest old plane in all God's sky
BB-gun for'd and a slingshot aft
Hundred twenty knots when in a forced draft.[1]

They came with confidence, their freshly painted, sooty-black aircraft looking very business-like and menacing. There were a few old hands among them, taken from other squadrons then operating in the Hawaiian Islands. But most of the pilots came directly from advanced flight training in the States and were as green as grass. They knew precious little of what had gone before them, of the near-annihilation of Patrol Wing 10, of the long agonizing retreat to Australia, or even of the tenuous foothold that had now been secured in the Solomons. Officers and enlisted men alike were long on enthusiasm but short on experience.

Patrol Squadron 54 had been established in November 1942 as a brand-new entity and three months later received orders to deploy to the South Pacific as a Black Cat squadron. Its planes took off from Kaneohe Bay in early March with little specialized training for the hazardous work that lay ahead. On the eleventh of that month, the first crews began arriving at Henderson Field to join forces with, and eventually to relieve, VP-12.

Perhaps the keystone of squadron confidence was its young, newly promoted commanding officer, Lieutenant Commander Carl W. Schoenweiss. He was a big man with blonde wavy hair and steel-blue eyes, and there was never any question who was in command or which way the squadron was going. He was a no-nonsense type and was out to do the Japanese as much damage as possible.

For the first two and a half months of the deployment, VP-54 shared Black Cat tasks with VP-12 and oriented themselves to the new night environment. They learned how to navigate among the islands by radar, how to make themselves invisible to enemy fighters, and how to sneak under bad weather at a few hundred feet while skirting volcanic peaks that rose abruptly from the sea.

Schoenweiss in one aircraft and Lieutenant (j.g.) Robert L. Engemann in another flew an orientation flight with pilots from VP-12 on the night of March 15. The two Cats spotted for a bombardment of Vila airfield by surface ships, and capped the action with 500-pound bombs. After the first few such flights, the pilots and crews of VP-54 were on their own.

On March 31, Schoenweiss with Lieutenant John W. Erhard as copilot made the first squadron contact with enemy surface ships, locating three destroyers west of Vella Lavella, the northwesternmost island in the New Georgia Group. A short time later these were joined by four more warships, making a total of two light cruisers and five destroyers. The Cat notified base radio and tracked the enemy force into Vella Gulf and along the coastline of Kolombangara until two Army B-24s arrived on the scene. The PBY then illuminated the ships with flares while the B-24s made unsuccessful bombing runs. The Japanese commander wisely decided that it was too risky to stop and attempt to offload his troops and supplies under the circumstances, and within only five miles of Vila he reversed course and headed for home. When the B-24s left, the Cat picked out a destroyer at the end of the column and made its own glide-bombing attack. Two 500-pound bombs straddled the vessel close aboard and may have done underwater damage. More important was the fact that the task force landed no troops or materiel that night.

Lieutenant (j.g.) James W. Anderson found another task force five nights later in the Blackett Strait, which skirts the southwest corner of Kolombangara. It was made up of a light cruiser, two destroyers, and two transports, also headed for Vila. Anderson elected to make an immediate bombing attack. As he made his run in, he was picked up by searchlights and heavy gunfire and was forced to turn away. Before he could make another run the destroyers laid thick smoke, under cover of which the transports landed their troops. Later the Cat attempted another attack as the force made a high-speed exit through Ferguson Passage. Anderson dropped two 500-pound bombs on one of the ships, with no discernible results.

During March, April, and May two planes were lost, one as a consequence of engine failure on takeoff and one as the result of an unexplained crash in the open sea by an aircraft on a Mike Search. During a subsequent attempt to locate the missing plane, Schoenweiss found a life raft and parachute but no sign of the crew. They had been swallowed by the great hungry ocean, which lies in wait for those who would skim over its surface in the black of the night.

The squadron was quartered in tents on the site of an old coconut plantation, under conditions as foul as those encountered by VP-12. Drainage was poor, despite efforts to dig ditches to carry water away from the tent area. It was the rainy season and the frequent downpours simply filled the ditches and overflowed into the camp. There was no flooring in the tents and VP-54 personnel literally lived in the mud.

The entire camp was surrounded by thick undergrowth, and mosquitoes plagued the men day and night. About twenty percent of squadron personnel suffered from chills, fever, and various manifestations of malaria, while some thirty-five percent evidenced symptoms of dysentery. At night "Washing Machine Charlie" flew over with regularity and foxholes were dug close to every tent. The more luxurious of these foxholes boasted canvas flaps to keep out the water. The squadron CO was determined to improve on these conditions—but how? Admiral Nimitz had decreed that Guadalcanal was *not* to become a permanent base and this was apparently enough to stymie any serious efforts to upgrade accommodations for deployed squadron personnel.

A visit to Guadalcanal by Secretary of the Navy Artemus Gates gave Schoenweiss the opening he was looking for. A VP-54 aircraft was assigned to fly the Secretary to the Russell Islands on an inspection trip, and the young skipper assigned himself as pilot. On the return trip Gates visited the cockpit and mentioned his intention to look in on some of the squadron camps at Henderson. Schoenweiss graciously invited him to the Black Cat Camp and the Secretary accepted.

That same afternoon Gates visited the VP-54 living area and was taken aback by the conditions there. Schoenweiss responded that things were rather pleasant then, but that he should see it after a heavy rain. That night there was just such a downpour and in the morning the Secretary returned to see if the young skipper had exaggerated his case. His question was answered as he slogged through the thick black mud.

Gates ordered that a new camp be built for the Cat squadron and directed that a report be submitted to him personally when that had been accomplished. Consequently, VP-54 and its support personnel moved into their new quarters on June 25. The camp consisted of newly constructed quonset huts, built on crushed coral in proximity to the field. Health, efficiency, and morale improved overnight.[2]

From the time of VP-54's arrival in mid-March to VP-12's departure on

104

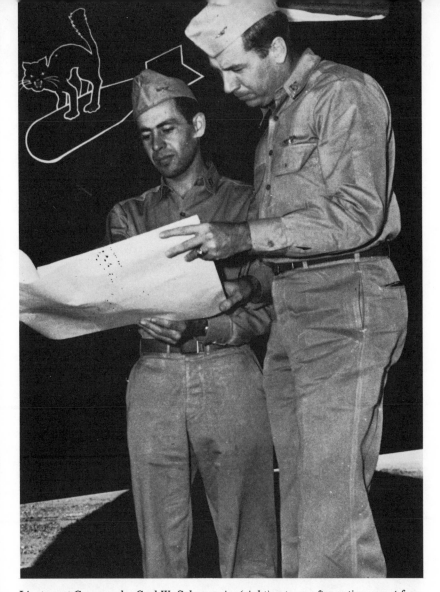

Lieutenant Commander Carl W. Schoenweiss (right) gets an after-action report from one of his pilots. VP-54's insignia, a Black Cat riding a bomb, looks down from the hull of a PBY. (Captain C. Schoenweiss collection)

the first of June, things had been relatively quiet in the Solomons. The enemy evacuation of Guadalcanal in February had signalled a lull of sorts while both sides decided what was to be done next. New battle lines had to be drawn before the fighting could begin again in earnest.

The Allies, as might be expected, were preparing to move against the Central Solomons. The Japanese, for their part, were determined to hold

105

that area and halt the Allied drive to the northwest. A new defensive line would be drawn from the Mariana Islands southeast to Truk and thence to the Central Solomons. There it would take a sharp turn to the west across the Solomon Sea to Salamaua in New Guinea and from there to Timor. While holding the line against the inevitable Allied onslaught, they would build new bases, reinforce existing ones, and gird themselves for an all-out offensive in the spring of 1944.

Rabaul, with its formidable base complex including several airfields, was the head of the octopus south of the equator. One tentacle reached toward New Guinea while another wound down through the Solomons chain with its bases and airstrips. These latter positions enabled the enemy to project his air power all the way to Guadalcanal, while anchorages and other facilities along the way provided staging areas for waterborne logistic support and surface sorties. The airfield at Buka Passage was only 165 miles from Rabaul, Kahili at the southern end of Bougainville and Ballale Island airstrip just offshore were stepping stones to Vila on Kolombangara, Munda on New Georgia, and Rekata Bay on Santa Isabel. The last mentioned was a seaplane base but the Japanese planned

VP-54 encampment during a rare dry spell. (Captain C. Schoenweiss collection)

One of the more luxurious foxholes, alongside a tent with a canvas flap to keep out the rain. (L. C. Hylton collection)

at least two more airfields on this island, all within easy striking distance of the American positions on Tulagi and Guadalcanal.

Vila and Munda were, of course, already in operation and the Japanese increased their efforts to expand and reinforce these important bases in spite of day and night bombings. The Black Cats of VP-54 made frequent

107

night visits to both these airfields, dropping 500-pound bombs, anti-personnel bombs, and other miscellaneous pieces.

Much of the ongoing construction at the two bases was accomplished at night. To counter this, the Black Cats modified some of their ordnance accordingly. Ground crews requisitioned a large number of steel rods ordinarily used in construction to reinforce concrete and secured them lengthwise to 500-pound bombs with metal straps. Then they extended another rod forward from the impact fuze in the nose of the weapon so it would detonate prematurely above ground. The flying metal from thousands of pieces of reinforcing rod was lethal to enemy personnel working within several hundred yards of the impact area. These improvisations were known as "daisy cutters."

Having softened up enemy positions at Munda and Vila by almost continuous day and night bombing for several weeks, the time for invasion arrived. On June 30, American forces landed on the northern end of Rendova Island, a few miles from Munda across the Blanche Channel.

Earlier in the month, when it became clear that the action was moving north, Schoenweiss requested and received permission to expand the Mike Search as far north as Bougainville. This gave the Cats an opportunity to intercept enemy ships at the top of the Slot and to give early warning to Allied forces dug in on Rendova and operating in smaller numbers on New Georgia. Between four and six Black Cats took off nightly, searching the Slot and the approaches to New Georgia for Japanese task forces headed south to bombard newly landed U.S. forces and to deliver troops and supplies to threatened Japanese positions.[3]

On the night of July 4–5, Lieutenant Commander Schoenweiss in one Cat and Lieutenant McDonough in another spotted for a task force which shelled Vila on Kolombangara, and Bairoko Harbor on the opposite side of Kula Gulf, in an effort to slow down the transfer of reinforcements by the enemy from Vila to Munda. Following the surface bombardments, McDonough put his four 500-pounders on Vila while Schoenweiss dropped his on Bairoko Harbor facilities.

Throughout the month VP-54 Black Cats searched out, reported, and attacked a number of enemy ships and task groups which were making their way south after dark in a concentrated attempt to break the Allied stranglehold on the Central Solomons. On the night of the 12th, a Cat flown by Lieutenants (j.g.) William E. Carter and Harry G. Sharp made its way up the Slot in search of the Tokyo Express. Concentrating its efforts in the area between New Georgia and the Shortland Islands, the Cat completed two and a half circuits before it made contact with the enemy just after midnight. The task force was located some fifteen miles north of Kolombangara and consisted of five destroyers led by the light cruiser *Jintsu*. It was coming on fast.

108

Admiral Halsey had received word earlier in the day that the Japanese formation was on its way south. He moved an Allied task force, commanded by Rear Admiral Walden L. "Pug" Ainsworth, into the area to intercept it. Carter's Cat quickly established communications with the Allied force, which was now only thirty-five miles distant, and guided it to the target. Sometime after 0100 the two opposing formations sighted each other and the Battle of Kolombangara was on.

American destroyers moved in first with torpedoes. The *Jintsu* responded with her big guns while attempting to illuminate the attacking vessels with her searchlight. Meanwhile Ainsworth's flagship the *Honolulu* moved in closer. Then she and two other cruisers opened fire. The Black Cat spotter circling above saw that the rounds were falling short of the target and advised the *Honolulu* to move them up 200 yards. Now the 6-inch projectiles began raining down on the hapless enemy cruiser with

VP-81 pilots receive briefing at Bougainville before a mission. (U.S. Navy)

deadly accuracy. The *Jintsu* was literally torn apart. The Cat crew could see the "explosions and flashes from her decks," and the Japanese warship went dead in the water.[4] The American destroyers then moved in smartly and drove two torpedoes into her. Suddenly she split into two flaming pieces and perished. It was a spectacular yet sobering sight.

But there was no time to sit and reflect on what had happened. Carter spotted four of the Japanese destroyers headed for a rain squall, reported his observation to the task force commander, and then went after them himself. Under cover of the weather the enemy ships split up, but Carter caught two of them coming out the other side of the squall, streaking up the Slot for home.

The Cat moved in and dropped two 500-pounders which missed completely. Return fire was heavy. On the second pass Carter released his remaining two heavies. It was a good try but there was no evidence he had scored. And the plane had been jolted by hits on the wings during the run in. It was impossible to determine the extent of the damage. Low on fuel and with ordnance expended, the Black Cat reluctantly headed for home. Arriving at Henderson some time later the crew inspected the damage to their aircraft and were astonished to find several large holes, three feet in diameter, in the starboard wing and a number of smaller ones in the port. From then on, the old Cat was viewed with new respect.

But despite its well-deserved reputation for reliability there were occasions when the PBY didn't make it all the way home. On one such night, July 16–17, Lieutenant (j.g.) Jim Anderson and his crew had searched the Slot to Bougainville and were headed south again. As they came abreast of Vella Lavella Island, the starboard engine began to act up and finally burst into flames. All attempts to extinguish the blaze failed and Anderson knew he would have to set the plane down in the open sea—and quickly. The fire was burning brightly now and he was concerned that it might reach the fuel in the wing tank.

As he made his hasty approach to touchdown, the fire reflected off the water and provided him with some visual reference. But it was not enough to permit him to determine the direction of the swells or the wind on the water's surface. Trusting to luck, he continued his descent.

The Cat hit hard and stuck. In fact it was such a jolt that the burning engine was torn from its mounts and fell sizzling into the water. Miraculously, they had not torn the bottom out of the airplane and it bobbed about on the waves. But Anderson and his crew were in a tight spot. Vella Lavella was occupied by the Japanese and they had almost certainly seen the burning airplane land in the open sea. Soon they would be out to investigate.

Quickly he ordered the crew into two rubber rafts. Then he made his

110

way aft to one of the .50-caliber waist guns. He turned the gun inward and riddled the Cat's bottom with holes. Now there was no time to waste. Having administered the *coup de grâce*, he climbed into one of the rafts. They began paddling furiously to put as much distance as possible between themselves and the sinking aircraft. Perhaps a half-hour later, a launch arrived on the scene and searched the area briefly. The Cat crew watched quietly from a distance. The Japanese apparently believed the burning airplane had crashed into the sea and the pilot had gone down with the wreckage. They soon gave up and headed for shore.

With the immediate danger past, the Cat crew now set out for the beach in hope they could make it before dawn. The next morning found the group on Vella Lavella making their way gingerly along the beach at the edge of the jungle. They had no idea what they might find, but they could not simply wait to be discovered or to starve to death. Suddenly they heard someone coming along a path to the beach. Aviation Radio Technician first class Doug Roberts remembers that "he was one of the fattest Japanese I have ever seen, before or since—Mr. five-by-five."[5] They decided to station themselves along the path and jump him when he returned.

But fate intervened again and before they could put their hastily made plan into action, two F4U Corsairs, whose pilots had no idea that Americans were down there, came in low and began strafing a large Japanese camp no more than a hundred yards into the jungle. Seeing their chance the Cat crew took off down the beach in the opposite direction and regrouped. Only one man, the plane captain, was missing. By this time the Corsairs had left and were winging their way out over the ocean toward home, still unaware of the drama that had taken place below.

While the Cat crew was wondering what to do next, they heard the missing crewman shout. Then there was a single shot and all was quiet. There was not much question what had happened.

Strangely enough the Japanese did not search the area. Perhaps they thought they had killed the pilot of the downed aircraft and that there was no one else about. Whatever the case, the Cat crew members put more distance between themselves and the enemy camp and then stopped to rest. Here fate interceded again.

That morning when they had first come ashore, one of the crewmen discarded his flight jacket in the brush. There a native found it and took it back to his village. The chief recognized it as belonging to an American and organized a search party.

A few hours later the crewmen saw the jungle foliage part, and before they could get to their handguns they were surrounded by natives. Through sign language and pidgin English the tribesmen made them-

111

selves understood. They were friends. They would take the Americans to a safe place.

Roberts says they then struck out on "a hell of a hike," ascending high up into the mountains.[6] After hours of climbing they finally came to a camp. There they were introduced to coastwatcher Leftenant Jocelyn of the Royal Navy. With him were four Samoans in blue uniforms. Things had begun to look up.

Jocelyn had a radio, of course, and soon made contact with the Americans at Guadalcanal who promised to dispatch a PT boat to pick up the Cat crew. A few nights later they left the camp just after dark and after six hours of walking broke out of the jungle onto the beach. Natives in dugout canoes were waiting for them to paddle them out to the PT boat waiting offshore. By next morning they were telling their story at Henderson Field.

During their absence the American troops had continued to tighten the noose on Munda. As might be expected, the Japanese on New Georgia fought back savagely. The Cats scoured the sea approaches looking for enemy surface units which regularly attempted to penetrate the area with skill and determination. Many got through to reinforce their comrades but some did not.

Lieutenant (j.g.) Fred Gage found what he described as a corvette-type combatant ship on the night of July 17 just northwest of Vella Lavella. He dropped all four of his 500-pounders on the ship. Unable to determine if any of his weapons had scored he returned to the target and strafed it with .30- and .50-caliber machine-gun fire. The vessel was afire and seemed to be wracked by an explosion as it disappeared into a front. Shortly afterward it disappeared from the radar scope and could not be located again.

At about 2230 on the 19th of July a VP-54 Cat, flown by Lieutenant Harold T. Johnson, made radar contact ten miles east of Fauro Island. It turned out to be a large enemy force of heavy and light cruisers, destroyers, and destroyer transports. Johnson reported their presence to base and tracked them south. Later, the formation divided in two, combatants remaining in the Slot to ambush any Allied task force which might be sent to intercept them, and the destroyer transports ducking into Vella Gulf to deliver their cargoes at Vila. The Cat had been patiently waiting for just such a chance to pounce. Johnson went after the destroyer transports.

Since the three ships were steaming in column the aircraft commander elected to approach from the rear and drop all his 500-pound bombs in a stick, one right after the other. That way, he reasoned, he had a good chance of hitting at least one.

112

Mechanics labored through the scorching heat of the day to keep the Cats in the air at night. (Captain G. Bogart collection)

113

Johnson made his approach throttled back and just before passing over the stern of the last ship called for the drop. The first bomb landed smack on the superstructure of tail-end Charlie, the second was a miss, and the third hit the fantail of the second ship in the column. The fourth bomb was also a miss. The PBY had encountered fierce antiaircraft fire from all three vessels and was badly damaged, but the two destroyer transports, while still under way, were streaming smoke. Johnson remained on station and directed other aircraft from Henderson. The enemy vessels turned and scattered and the battered Cat returned to Henderson, arriving just before daylight to lick its wounds and prepare to fight again.

One of the interesting new sideline activities performed by the Black Cats during this period was the gathering of intelligence information on enemy radar installations. While Allied electronic detection capability was well ahead of that of the Japanese, U.S. experts had become concerned in August 1942 by concrete evidence in that Japanese radar technology had developed to the point where it now became a threat to U.S. surface operations in the South Pacific. The hard fact of the matter was that the enemy had at least one working unit in operation at this time on Guadalcanal:

This radar was captured when the Marines landed. It was running, hot and not damaged and located on the inland end of Henderson Field. This installation was dismantled and taken to the Naval Research Laboratory (NRL) in Washington, D.C. for evaluation. It was a surface search, 90 mc radar, I believe, with a bedspring antenna. NRL evaluated the equipment and developed a passive intercept receiver (XARD-1) and an airborne jammer to counter similar systems.[7]

Six enlisted men who had just completed Radio Material School (Class 40) and had received training in the embryonic new field of electronic countermeasures were assigned to take this new equipment to the Solomons and find out just how far the Japanese had developed their capability.* This was the start of Cast Mike Project #1 (CM) whose purpose was to locate other enemy radar installations in the area.

Churchill and his group first installed their equipment in B-17 Flying Fortresses flying out of Espirito Santo. These flights produced nothing and by December 1942, Churchill had moved the operation to Guadalcanal. In early January the group began operating with the Black Cats of VP-12 and later did much of their work with VP-54.

*The six men on this project were ACRM Jack G. Churchill, ACRM Stanley P. Von Achen, ACRT William Pueschel, ART1 William Russell, ART1 Douglas H. Roberts, and ARM1 J. Twombley.

A VP-44 Black Cat delivers supplies to coastwatchers. (Captain G. Bogart collection)

The electronic-countermeasures project was incidental to the regular missions of the Black Cats. The men who operated the special equipment also served in regular crew capacities, manning guns and providing whatever other services were needed. At first there was little evidence of additional Japanese radar installations in the area, but on a June 18 search-and-bombing mission up the Slot, radar emissions were detected coming from the Shortland Islands, just south of Bougainville. Other indications came from this area on July 10 but the station could not be pinpointed. On August 8 a VP-54 Cat flown by Lieutenant John W. Erhard obtained four good signals and the evidence began to point to Morgusaia Island in the Shortlands. But other attempts to confirm this were inconclusive.

Location of the station was questionable since we did not have a direction finding (DF) capability. Modification was made to an ASV radar receiver/lobing unit to permit it to operate on 190 mc. The CM crew with the assistance of the squadron metal benders fabricated a pair of ¼ wave Yagis [Antennae] which were mounted on the port and starboard side of the PBY-5A hull and connected to the ASV receiver and lobe switching unit. With this set up we were able to DF or home in on the signal . . . .[8]

115

On the night of September 8 another VP-54 Cat flown by Lieutenant Johnson was able to obtain three good bearings which pinpointed the Japanese station on Poporang Island just south of Bougainville. In confirming the location of this installation the Cat received a warm welcome with intense but fortunately inaccurate antiaircraft fire. The information was turned over to the Army Air Force, and P-39 aircraft laid waste to the station during daylight hours.

The Japanese were now employing barges extensively to move troops and supplies among the Solomon Islands. There were many advantages to using these vessels, as opposed to large surface ships. First of all, they were of shallow draft and could move along the shore of an island, where their presence was likely to be obscured by the land mass and thus shielded from the searching eyes of Black Cat radar. Further they could quickly disgorge their contents directly onto the beach without undue delay. And finally, they permitted the enemy to move his assets in small "packages" so that the loss of one was not catastrophic to the total effort.

The Black Cats offset this tactic by finding and attacking many. At about 0200 on the morning of September 23, Lieutenant (j.g.) Anderson's Cat picked up two barges making their way carefully along the long coastline of Choiseul Island. He made twelve strafing runs scoring many hits. The Japanese attempted to escape by beaching the craft. A coastwatcher later reported that upon reaching shore, the survivors "ran screaming and screeching into the jungle."[9] Later that month Lieutenant Erhard and his crew located ten of these barges also moving down the coast of Choiseul. It was a rerun of Anderson's experience. After repeated strafing, the barges were beached and those occupants who were able fled into the bush.

The barges were not completely unprotected and often responded with a barrage of machine-gun fire. Lieutenant J. T. Casey's plane was hit several times by irate Japanese gunners on the night of October 6 before it drove two of these vessels ashore, killing and wounding a number of their occupants. About two weeks later Lieutenant Anderson found a group of twenty-eight barges which he strafed repeatedly, doing a considerable amount of damage. Then he proceeded up the coast of Choiseul until he came upon a large cargo vessel which he bombed and strafed, leaving it sinking by the stern.

By the end of October it was time to move further up the ladder toward Rabaul. U.S. aircraft were already operating from the old Japanese airfield on Munda and from the new Barakoma Field built by the Americans on Vella Lavella. Allied forces made landings in the Treasury Islands to the south of Bougainville and on Choiseul to the southeast on October 27. On the night of October 31–November 1 a surface force with eyes provided by Black Cat spotters blasted the two enemy airfields at Buka Passage. The Marines went ashore at Cape Torokina on Empress Augusta Bay the following morning. Black Cats provided search and antisubmarine protection for the invading forces. It was an active period, during which another PBY aircraft was lost when it hit the water and broke up on impact. There were only two survivors who were picked up by a destroyer.

By mid-November the Marines' position on Bougainville was reasonably secure and the Seabees had begun work on the Torokina airfield, from which Allied air power would be projected still further to the northwest. By the end of the month the Black Cats had extended their searches well beyond Buka, which was still held by the Japanese, all the way to the St. George's Channel which divides New Ireland from New Britain.

On December 1, 1943, VP-54 turned over its Black Cat responsibilities to VP-81. During VP-54's tour in the Solomons its men had flown 376 night missions logging 3,204 combat hours. They had bombed and strafed a number of enemy vessels, sinking some and damaging several more. And in the process, they had rescued fifty-two men from downed aircraft in the open sea. In a matter of months the green, inexperienced crews that had flown out of Kaneohe Bay in March of that year had become experienced combat veterans. And they had been active participants in the drive up the Solomons chain.

VP-81 under Lieutenant Commander Eugene P. Rankin found that trafic in large enemy ships had diminished considerably from what it had been in previous months. But there was now increased barge activity to compensate for this and the Cats made the most of all opportunities presented.

While Allied forces had secured a foothold on Bougainville, the fighting was far from over. A defensive perimeter had been established and airfields were under construction from which American air power could be projected still further to the northwest. But the Japanese still held most of the island, including airfields to the north and south of the Allied position. At night, enemy barge convoys loaded with troops and supplies moved along the coast of Bougainville and disgorged their cargoes in the vicinity of Torokina for an offensive which would come in March, and for other later attempts. The Black Cats intercepted many of these nocturnal travellers and severely limited the enemy's ability to move troops freely even by this method.

VP-81 began its operations from Henderson Field, as had VP-12 and VP-54 before them, and ranged as far north as the St. George's Channel. By the beginning of February, however, they had moved up to Munda

Artwork on the hull of a VP-44 Black Cat. (Captain G. Bogart collection)

airfield on New Georgia. From there they flew night bombing missions against enemy shore installations and supply points. On March 4 they made two daylight raids on Japanese troop concentrations on Choiseul.

During that month the enemy made concentrated efforts to break through the Allied perimeter on Bougainville, but failed. Nevertheless, the barge traffic continued at a rapid pace, and the Black Cats teamed up with the PT boats to wreak havoc on these logistical links which had now become essential to enemy forces on Bougainville. Japanese reinforcements into the Torokina area slowed to a trickle and by May had been, for the most part, choked off. On the 7th VP-81 moved up and began its operations from Piva Yoke, one of the newly built airstrips on Bougainville.[10]

Meanwhile, VP-44 under Lieutenant Commander Gerard S. "Gerry" Bogart had been operating out of Espiritu Santo since March. This squadron, also equipped with amphibious PBY-5A aircraft, operated from Luganville airfield, a crushed coral strip which had been wrenched from the dense jungle. Bogart remembers that

> It was like landing in a canyon lined on each side with 150-foot mahogany trees covered with jungle vines. The sun could not penetrate to the forest floor except where the Sea Bees had slashed and carved the landscape with their intrepid bulldozers.[11]

118

In mid-February 1944 the Green Islands had been seized by Allied forces without much difficulty. This new base was located about halfway between the Allied position on Bougainville and the Japanese base at Rabaul. The Sea Bees had begun construction of a 4,000-foot airfield on one of the Green Islands shortly after the landing, and a month later American planes were operating from this strip and plastering enemy positions at Kavieng on New Ireland Island. VP-44 moved up and began operations from the Green Islands on June 15, 1944.

The Black Cats of VP-44 were key players in keeping the Japanese off-balance. Their most important task was to prevent the enemy from effecting force buildups on Bougainville and other bypassed islands. This meant a continuing assault on barge traffic and night bombing raids on Japanese airfields and other shore installations. Rabaul, now less than 150 miles away, was under continuous attack by Army, Navy, and Marine Corps aircraft. In addition, to their own night harassment raids the Black Cats were often called upon for rescue services.

Fighter response from Rabaul had diminished considerably by this time but had not been completely eliminated. Sometime after midnight on August 28, Lieutenant (j.g.) Lloyd W. Garrison made contact with a Jake floatplane aircraft (Aichi E13A) about eight miles southwest of Cape St. George, New Ireland. The enemy plane made a run on the Cat, closing to about seventy-five yards and passing underneath. Garrison swung the PBY hard to port and its bow and port gunners got a clear shot at the enemy as he streaked by. Flames burst from the cowling of the Japanese plane and moments later it plunged into shallow water off Lumbon Island. The following morning Garrison returned to the spot, with two F-4U fighters for cover, and photographed the wreckage.[12]

The Green Islands were home to VP-44 until mid-April 1945. Detachments operated from Torokina on Bougainville, and later from other bases along the path of the Allied advance, all the way to the Philippines. At one point this squadron had detachments deployed from the Fijis to Luzon.

Metamorphosis

It is now necessary to backtrack somewhat to describe the beginnings of a separate Black Cat effort which began in Australia.

It may be recalled that in March 1942 the ragged remnants of PAT-WING 10 had reached southwest Australia after an agonizing retreat which had begun in the Philippines. With only three aircraft remaining out of a total of forty-five, they began rebuilding their organization while engaging in antisubmarine operations off the west coast of Australia. This was a time when the enemy still had considerable momentum and there was much concern that he would soon invade Australia itself. As it turned out, the Japanese had no intention of dissipating their strength on the enormous Australian land mass. In any case, General MacArthur's forces stopped them in New Guinea and they were never able to realize their objective of taking Port Moresby. Indeed, after Midway and subsequent Allied operations in the Solomons, it began to become apparent that the Japanese war machine had stalled. The Allies began transitioning to an offensive mode of operations and the faithful old Catalina was one of the first to be moved up into the fray.

Construction began on a PBY repair base at Palm Island, Australia, and an advanced base at Samarai, New Guinea, in June 1943. By August of that year, the seaplane tender *San Pablo* (AVP-30) had arrived at Namoia Bay near Samarai and set up operations with PBY-5s of VP-101. Nightly searches were prescribed for the Solomon Sea and the Bismarck Sea west of Talasea. Twice weekly the PBYs searched the northern coast of New Guinea as far as Wewak.

The Royal Australian Air Force had been engaged in similar activities in this area, flying their Catalinas all the way from Cairns, Australia. They provided familiarization flights for the American pilots to get them quickly into the problem. It was an unusually long haul to the operating area and one Black Cat pilot vividly recalled his introductory ride.

They loaded ammo and flares on the catwalk so high . . . that you could not move around. We were so heavy, we ran three or four miles to get off. Then we stayed at about 500 feet in a nose up attitude and remained constantly at 95 knots. When fuel burned off and speed increased, the skipper reached up and pulled the power back a bit. All hands flew in khaki shorts. We slept until nightfall when we got into the enemy area and then began looking for targets. I do not recall what we did that night but do recall we were empty and nose down on the way back. Back at Cairns we had been in the air for 24 hours and 10 minutes.[1]

Other American PBY squadrons were also earmarked for Black Cat operations in the New Guinea area. VP-11, which had cut its teeth in the Solomons fracas, now moved west. They would be followed by VP-52, VP-33, and VP-34. All came under Fleet Air Wing 17 which was formed on September 15 as an administrative umbrella for Seventh Fleet aircraft. Commodore Thomas S. Combs who was Commander, Aircraft Seventh Fleet, was also double-hatted as the first commander of the wing, while the COs of the tenders from which the PBYs operated became the Task Group Commanders. But this part of the Pacific belonged to the Army, and General George C. Kenney exercised overall operational control of all land-based air forces (including tender-based PBYs). Whereas Admiral Fitch's air forces in the Solomons traced their chain of command through Commander South Pacific Forces to Admiral Nimitz in Pearl Harbor, Commodore Combs' PBYs operated in the Southwest Pacific theater under General MacArthur.

At first the primary mission of VP-101 was to search the area in the vicinity of the Trobriand Islands in the Solomon Sea. The Allies had landed troops on Woodlark and Kiriwina Islands in this group in June, and a Japanese response to this move was considered likely. Such a response was not forthcoming, however, and PBY coverage was soon expanded to the northeast to include the shipping lane between Rabaul and Buka Passage. If the Catalinas found suitable targets they were instructed to notify base radio so that planes from the Fifth Air Force could be sent to make the strike. The PBY pilots were enjoined from making independent attacks "unless there was little danger to fear from enemy countermeasures."[2]

121

The seaplane tender San Pablo *at Namoia Bay, New Guinea. Planes are moored nearby in the buoy patch. (Ward H. Tanzer collection)*

The searches were indeed fruitful, particularly between Rabaul and Buka, and major targets were detected on more than half of the flights. The Cats dutifully sent out their contact reports as instructed, but for reasons which are not entirely clear, the Army bombers never arrived on the scene. The result was that the Japanese moved troops and cargo freely through this area with little difficulty. During this period only barges and small cargo vessels seemed to fit the requirements for attack, and the Cats vented their frustrations on these.

The seaplane tender *Half Moon*, (AVP 26) arrived at Namoia Bay on October 6 to relieve the *San Pablo* and began conducting operations with VPB-11* on the 9th. The *Half Moon*'s skipper, Commander W. O. "Bill" Gallery, quickly realized the folly of the search-and-report procedure.

*All Patrol Squadrons were redesignated Patrol Bombing Squadrons (VPB) on October 1, 1944.

The planes were expending much effort but had little to show for it. Something would have to be done about it.

On the night of October 11, Lieutenant (j.g.) T. L. "Tom" Hine found and attacked a surfaced submarine off the southern coast of New Britain. He apparently felt that it offered little danger to the PBY, and therefore fit the attack criteria. As the Cat bore in on the target the submarine skipper executed a crash dive to escape. At an altitude of about 200 feet Hine released two depth charges with hydrostatic fuzes. One of these landed just ahead of the swirl made by the disappearing sub and exploded seconds later. The other exploded on impact with the water, and the force of the blast shattered the tail section of the aircraft. Much of the elevator was blown away and a major portion of the horizontal stabilizer was bent upward at a forty-five degree angle.

There are limits to what even a PBY can do under such circumstances. It was evident that the aircraft could no longer sustain flight and Hine struggled to retain enough control to set her down in the open sea. Using the engines and the control surfaces which continued to respond, he fought the staggering Cat down to what ordnanceman Howard R. Kenyon remembers as "a beautiful night landing."[3] The airplane sank almost immediately, but there was enough time to break out two rubber life rafts into which the crew quickly scrambled.

All were accounted for and no one had been hurt, but they were now down in the open sea no more than four or five miles south of the enemy base at Gasmata, New Britain. The Japanese sent out boats to search for them but they escaped detection in the darkness. Hine concluded that to go ashore on the enemy-held island would almost certainly result in death or capture. He decided to strike out for Kiriwina Island some 150 miles to the south. By daylight they were well out to sea.

For almost three full days and nights they paddled while their squadron mates searched for them. Once, on the night of October 13, Lieutenant K. L. "Ken" MacWhinney and his crew passed directly over the boats but did not see them. Hine decided against firing his Very pistol for feat that the aircraft was Japanese. On they paddled.

When they were only sixty miles north of Kiriwina they were spotted by an Australian Air Force plane and rescued a short time later by a U.S. OA-10A aircraft, the Army version of the PBY-5A. Hine and his crew were happy to be picked up but proudly noted that they would have made it all the way under their own power in another two days.

Back at the tender, operations continued as before. Former All-American football star Lieutenant W. E. "Walt" Shinn found a tug and its tow in the Dampier Strait on the night of the 16th and bombed it. Lieutenant J. D. "Jack" Cruze attacked five enemy barges that same night with fragmentation bombs and low-altitude strafing. One barge sank, two were run up onto a reef and abandoned, and the remaining two were badly damaged. Three nights later, Cruze strafed enemy shore installations and several barges at Wide Bay, New Britain. The plane was riddled by light antiaircraft fire in this engagement but no one was injured.

Everyone was acutely aware that there was bigger game for the taking. As Task Group Commander, Gallery was becoming increasingly frustrated over the waste of assets and the opportunities missed due to restrictions imposed by higher command. Many of the crews felt the same way and some of the more aggressive plane commanders were chafing at the bit to try something new. Gallery decided to initiate a series of experiments in which various attack techniques were evaluated.

In the early-morning hours of October 24, Lieutenant (j.g.) L. M. "Nelly" Nelson found a good opportunity to attack a real enemy with long fangs. Nelson and the crew of his Cat "Black Magic" were patrolling the southern coast of New Britain looking for game, when at 0248 the radar operator picked up two contacts inside Japanese-held Jacquinot Bay. Nelson decided to have a look and shortly thereafter came upon two destroyers moving across the Bay at high speed, one behind the other, with wakes stretching out for a mile astern. Ensign John Sullivan was in the forward bombing compartment. He recalls that they were met with heavy antiaircraft fire when they entered the bay; "all hell broke loose— not only from the destroyers but also from the shore installation."[4] In retrospect, he believes they survived the hail of fire only because the Japanese calculated the PBY's speed as faster than it really was. "They [the tracers] seemed to be heading for my eyes but always preceded the nose of the aircraft."[5]

On they came at 1,000 feet, and Sullivan set up for a level drop using a somewhat crude grid sighting mechanism. As he drew a bead on the rear destroyer it made an evasive turn which distorted the solution. Nelson immediately pushed the nose over and dove for the lead ship which had now turned almost broadside to the attacking aircraft. Antiaircraft fire was intense from both destroyers, a third ship in the distance, and shore batteries. Nelson took aim by seaman's eye and released two 500-pound bombs when it looked just right. One of these found its mark on a particularly vulnerable spot near the after stack and exploded. The aircraft went into a steep bank to the right to escape the antiaircraft fire and retired out of range. A short time later the Cat made one more run to inspect its handiwork. The destroyer *Mochizuki* was ablaze from amidships to stern and dead in the water. Although mortally wounded she continued to fire her forward guns in defiance as Black Magic made

124

New Guinea
and the Bismarck Archipelago

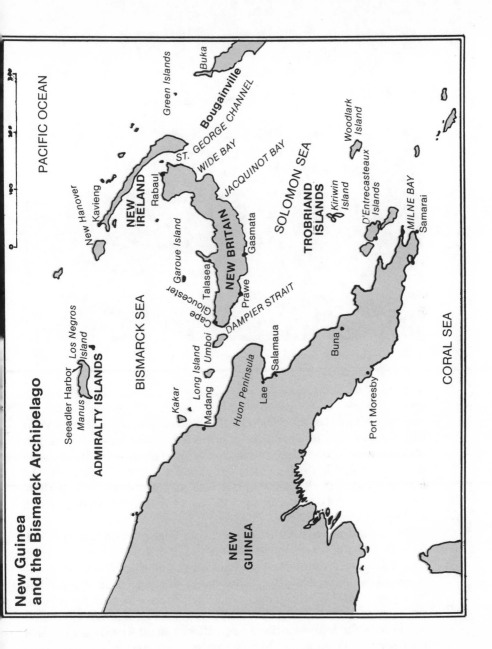

PACIFIC OCEAN

Green Islands

Buka

Bougainville

ST. GEORGE CHANNEL

WIDE BAY

JACQUINOT BAY

Woodlark Island

Kiriwin Island

D'Entrecasteaux Islands

SOLOMON SEA

TROBRIAND ISLANDS

MILNE BAY

Samarai

New Hanover

Kavieng

NEW IRELAND

Rabaul

Garoue Island

NEW BRITAIN

Gasmata

Talasea

Cape Gloucester

Prawe

DAMPIER STRAIT

BISMARCK SEA

Seeadler Harbor

Los Negros Island

Manus

ADMIRALTY ISLANDS

Kakar

Long Island

Madang

Umboi

Huon Peninsula

Lae

Salamaua

Buna

Port Moresby

NEW GUINEA

CORAL SEA

Black Cats outbound, looking for trouble. (U.S. Navy)

its final pass. The second destroyer was observed withdrawing at high speed.

The sinking of the *Mochizuki* by Black Magic seemed to confirm what Bill Gallery and others already suspected. Warships—even heavily armed warships travelling in company—could be successfully attacked at night by PBYs. In this particular case the firepower of the two destroyers and a third enemy vessel was augmented by that of shore batteries. But the Cat had made its kill nonetheless, and came back with all hands to tell about it.

Gallery did not request permission from higher command to switch from search-and-report to search-and-attack missions. Such a request would almost certainly have become bogged down in the maze of the cumbersome Army/Navy organizational structure. If an answer had been immediately forthcoming, it was likely to have been unfavorable. It was time for a decision by the on-scene commander and Gallery took it upon himself to authorize the change. Black Cat pilots were not *directed* to attack enemy shipping—but understood that they had his permission and backing to do so if the opportunity presented itself. Bill Gallery had really stuck his neck out this time—way out! The Cat crews knew the chance he was taking. But he was a man with the courage of his convictions and he was willing to do what was necessary to get the job done. Risk-taking, after all, is a hazard of command. One VPB-11 officer remembers him as "the finest naval officer I or anyone else ever knew."[6]

Every morning at 0800, pilots assigned to fly that night ordered the bomb loads they wanted. A standard load was developed, consisting of two 1,000-pound and two 500-pound general-purpose bombs, with tail fuzes set for four to five seconds delay. Nose fuzes were set for 1/10 of a second, but were not generally armed for attacks below 1,000 feet. The chance of destroying one's own aircraft was too great.

Ideally the attack was made down the length of the ship from either a bow or stern aspect. Bombs were released by use of an intervalometer with a recommended setting of 75 feet spacing at a calculated altitude of 200 feet at the time of drop. The order of release was one 500-pounder, followed by each of the two 1,000-pound bombs, and finally by the last 500. This meant that if only one of the four bombs found its mark, it was more likely to be one of the 1,000-pounders. A pilot, however, could release the weapons one or two at a time if he preferred, and often did so

Commander Bill Gallery (bottom row center) and the crew of "Black Magic." Lieutenant (j.g.) Nelson is on Gallery's right and Ensign Sullivan is on his left. (Lieutenant Commander John E. Sullivan collection)

as the situation dictated. Most important of all, however, was the realization that the closer one got to the target, the better were his chances of success—and survival. Pilots like Jack Cruze, who were strong advocates of the masthead level attack, were ready and willing to demonstrate the clear advantages of this technique. The bombsight was eventually discarded altogether as a useless piece of baggage.

The Black Cats were now hunters in a very real sense, but during the first ten nights of operating under the new policy no hits were scored. Lieutenant Goodwyn R. "Goody" Taylor attacked two enemy destroyers off Kavieng on New Ireland Island on the night of October 26 and his aircraft was holed in several places by antiaircraft fire. His bombs straddled his intended victim but did no damage. Lieutenant Jack Penfold went after an 8,000-ton tanker on November 9 but scored only with small fragmentation bombs. Damage was superficial.[7]

Then on November 14, things began to happen. At about 0200 on that date Walt Shinn located a three-ship formation off New Britain headed for Rabaul. There were three ships: a light cruiser, a large cargo vessel, and a smaller ship of undetermined type. Shinn lined up and made a low-level bombing run on the large merchant ship, releasing his full load. As luck would have it, one 1,000-pound bomb failed to drop and the other three bombs missed the target. Undismayed, Shinn turned and made another pass, this time at the cruiser. When in position he pulled the release handle and the 1,000-pounder left the aircraft, hit the ship aft of the stacks, and exploded below deck. Shinn was then driven away by intense antiaircraft fire and the arrival of enemy night fighters. The ultimate result of the attack could not be determined but it was clear that the enemy cruiser had been badly hurt.

At about the same time, Jack Penfold came upon a convoy of one large and two smaller cargo-type ships. One of his 500-pounders struck the superstructure of the 1,000-ton vessel amidships, causing a large flash and a considerable amount of flying debris.

On the 16th, Lieutenant (j.g.) Haas found a convoy consisting of two cargo vessels, one destroyer and one patrol craft. He radioed a contact report and proceeded to attack. Although his bombs did not find their marks, Lieutenant Jack Cruze had intercepted Haas' contact report and hurried to assist. Arriving on the scene a short time later, Cruze picked out one of the cargo types and placed two bombs, one 1,000-pounder and one smaller bomb, squarely on the unfortunate vessel and left her sinking.

Lieutenant Taylor experimented with a night torpedo attack in the early-morning hours of the 18th at a drop altitude of 125 feet. The torpedo passed across the ship's bow and as the Cat passed by the enemy vessel,

128

an oil line was shot out on the PBY's port engine, necessitating feathering. Taylor and his crew made it to Kiriwina Island on the starboard engine, none the worse for their experience.

On the 20th, Jack Penfold came upon a six-ship convoy on the southwest side of New Ireland about halfway between Rabual and Kavieng. He scored three direct hits on a 10,000-ton cargo ship with two 1,000-pounders and one 500-pounder. When he departed the area the ship was burning fiercely and the flames could be seen many miles away.[8]

By this time it was clear that Bill Gallery's gamble had paid off. Armed with the impressive results of his audacity, Gallery presented his case to Commodore Combs. Here was a chance to hit the enemy where it would hurt—to chew up his vital supply links, to maul even his warships, and to sap his morale. Combs was responsive to Gallery's reasoning and from that time forward, it was official. Henceforth, the primary mission of the Black Cats in the Southwest Pacific would be search and *attack*.

10

The Stuff of Legends

Oh the radar revealed a Nippy cruiser
A might bruiser but sure the loser
Cause ol' Fifty-two was now a-coming
With engines humming
To deal with same

From the *PBY Serenade*,
Patrol Bombing Squadron 52

VPB-11 had done its job well and was now transferred to Port Moresby where its planes were assigned to convoy and rescue duty. On December 16 the squadron was called upon to evacuate an Australian Army unit stranded in the New Guinea hinterland and threatened by the approach of Japanese forces. The enemy was closing in rapidly and the Cats were the Australians' only hope of escape.

It was mountainous territory and the Cats were obliged to snake in through fog-shrouded valleys to land in the upper reaches of the Sepik River. The water was quite shallow at the landing site and the river there was no more than two wing spans in width. The land rose abruptly on each side. One of the first planes to make the trip in through the mountains was that of the squadron CO, Lieutenant Commander C. M. "Scotty" Campbell. Lieutenant Wesley "Wes" Van Benschoten and Lieutenant T. H. Ragsdale joined in. Five days and seventeen trips later, some 219 Australians, their equipment, and a number of friendly natives had been airlifted out. Ragsdale made the last flight in and took out the rear guard as the Japanese closed in on the abandoned outpost.[1]

Back at Palm Island, Australia, Patrol Bombing Squadron 52 under Lieutenant Commander H. A. "Hal" Sommer had been readying itself to move north and relieve VPB-11. Here, one of the war's more colorful Black Cat pilots, Lieutenant W. J. "Bill" Lahodney, was deeply involved in a project which he hoped would substantially increase the striking power of the Catalina. Something was needed, he felt, to enable a Cat to press home an attack even after all bombs or torpedoes had been expended. Further, he knew that they would encounter many targets, too small to waste bombs on, which would succumb to an attack by concentrated gunfire.

In his quest for increased firepower, Lahodney made several flights in the Army's B-25 bombers and was impressed with their gunfire capabilities. These planes had 75-millimeter cannon in the nose but also mounted several fixed-quad .50-caliber machine guns which were of particular interest to the Cat pilot. He decided to experiment with the same .50-caliber installation in the nose of his PBY. It was a somewhat radical concept and, as might be expected, there were many raised eyebrows. The PBY after all was a patrol plane, not a fighter, and it was the opinion of some that the fifties would tear the nose off the airplane. The old Cat was simply not built to take that kind of abuse, they said. Others thought the installation would have an adverse affect on aircraft weight and balance. Few were optimistic that the idea would work.

Lahodney was not to be deterred. Removing the bombsight (which had not proven very effective for the specialized work of the Black Cats) and the small bow plate window, he bolted the guns, mounted two over two, to the keel of the big boat. The top set of two were mounted forward of the lower set, so the muzzles of all four were aft of the angled bow plate. An aluminum panel with four blast tubes extending forward for seven inches replaced the window, and was all that was visible of the lethal addition from an exterior view. An electric trigger on the pilot's yoke, and a selector switch which permitted the pilot to fire the guns individually or together, completed the installation. Bill Lahodney was confident that the Cat would not only withstand the vibration of the fifties, but that the twin thirties normally mounted just above that spot could be retained along with the gunner's position.

With a minimum volunteer crew, consisting of himself, a flight engineer, and a bow gunner, Lahodney took off from the Palm Island seadrome to try out his idea. Dropping a floating smoke light in the water for a target, he executed a wing-over and put the Cat into a steep dive. Eyeballing the burning smoke light he pressed the trigger and the fifties responded with a burst that churned the water and extinguished the smoke. That was the kind of firepower he was looking for, he thought

131

Lahodney's guns. Four fixed .50-caliber machine guns bolted to the keel proved lethal to enemy barges and other vessels. (Captain W. J. Lahodney collection)

with satisfaction. During the run he had also noted that the extra weight in the nose had no perceptible effect on the aircraft's performance. The test was repeated with the same result and upon returning to base, a careful inspection revealed that the old Cat had shouldered her new burden without complaint. The experiment was a complete success, so much so that quad fifties were installed in at least three planes in every succeeding squadron.[2]

Other tests also bore out Lahodney's views. They demonstrated that a gunner could straddle the quad mount and operate the thirties with almost as much mobility as before. A burlap pad was placed on top of the hot .50-caliber barrels to prevent the gunner from being burned.

One problem with the installation was that because of its positioning it was difficult to keep salt water from getting into the muzzles. Rubber plugs were made to fit in the blast tubes but they leaked badly. Then someone got the idea that the standard rubber devices used for the prevention of venereal disease would be just the thing to make the blast tubes watertight. And they were.

In preparing for the coming deployment, Lahodney flew over to Townsville on the Australian mainland on a supply run. He picked up two

132

additional quad mounts from the Army Supply Depot and an unusually large quantity of condoms to protect the gun muzzles. The swells were heavy that day and during the take-off run one bounced the Cat into the air prematurely. The starboard wing dropped about forty degrees and full power on the starboard engine would not bring it level. It hit the water and broke off and the rest of the airplane came down hard. As it began to sink, Lahodney again applied full throttle and ran the broken Cat up on the rocks of the Townsville breakwater. Incredibly, no one was hurt.

With a heavy on-shore wind, the condoms were scattered about and it looked like there were many thousands as they floated ashore. Lahodney recalls that since there were no women on Palm Island there was much humorous speculation concerning the intended use of all those contraceptives.[3]

On November 20, VPB-52 arrived at Namoia Bay to begin night operations against the Japanese. Action came quickly. On the night of the 22nd, Bill Lahodney and his crew located a destroyer escort off New Ireland and attacked it in a dive-bombing run. All four bombs missed the ship. A short time later, however, they picked up a barge in the St. George's Channel between Duke of York Island and New Ireland. Diving on the hapless victim, the Cats sent tracers from their quad fifties slamming into it the enemy craft, leaving it broken and burning. At least they would not go home empty-handed. Perhaps next time out, they would do better.

The Squadron Executive Officer, Lieutenant J. M. "Buck" Arbuckle, had an even more stimulating adventure that night. At about 2300 he found a small coastal vessel and decided to attack with strafing runs. There was no return gunfire and the enemy ship seemed an easy victim. Suddenly from nowhere they were taken under fire, perhaps from an unseen escort. One of the rounds hit the parachute flares piled in the after station and within seconds the fuselage all the way forward to the navigator's table was a flaming inferno. Arbuckle knew that there were fragmentation bombs back there which could tear the aircraft apart. With the entire crew crowded forward to escape the searing heat, Arbuckle set the Cat down in the water as quickly as he could. The life rafts had already been consumed by the fire and all hands simply jumped into the water. The bombs were still slung under the wings and Arbuckle was afraid they would detonate when the fire reached them. He ordered everyone to swim quickly away from the burning Cat but to keep together.

When they had reached what seemed to be a safe distance away from the Cat in her funeral pyre, Arbuckle began to concern himself with the

133

enemy ship or ships they had engaged. At this point all eleven crewmen had managed to stay together. All were uninjured, all had lifevests and were in no danger of drowning. And they were only 12 to 15 miles from New Ireland. The danger was that the Japanese would find them in the water and take them prisoner. But the Japanese never came. Arbuckle speculated that they were chased away by the activities of Bill Lahodney, who was also operating in that general area.

The little group now struck out for New Ireland. It was slow going, and by morning they were still a considerable distance from shore. With daylight came a new threat. A school of large fish with high dorsal fins were swimming about, in ever-closing patterns. As they moved in and began brushing against the men in the water, it was observed with relief that the antagonists were only porpoises.

At this point, several members of the crew wanted to stop, float, and rest for an indefinite period. Others insisted on going on. They decided at this point to split up. Arbuckle, his copilot, and one other crewman made the beach at about 1100 that morning. Then as their strength began to return, they staggered into the cover of the jungle.

Arbuckle decided that their best course of action was to try to make contact with the Australian coastwatchers, who operated in the hills and kept a few steps ahead of the Japanese patrols. They struck off through the undergrowth, avoiding paths which might be used by the Japanese. That night they slept in the jungle, nursing their sores and sharing their blood with mosquitoes.

In the morning they tried eating some unrecognizable fruit but found it bitter and unpalatable. They had now had enough of working their way through the jungle and elected to try a little-used path. They soon came upon an elderly native and found they could converse with him in pidgin English. Yes, he knew the Australians. Yes, he knew where they could be found. They were to follow him and he would lead them to safety. They followed along behind the old man for 15 to 20 minutes. It was a stroke of luck that they had found him. Perhaps they would make it yet. As they rounded a bend in the trail, a dozen or more Japanese soldiers with rifles surrounded them. It was all over.

The group was taken to Kavieng and later to Rabaul where they were reunited with other crew members who had also made it to shore and been captured. At this point eight out of the original crew of eleven had survived. Later, seven members of the Cat crew were put aboard ship to be taken to another prisoner-of-war camp. They were never heard from again. Arbuckle, Pappy Boyington (who had been shot down in action off Rabaul on January 3, 1944), and other prisoners who had been gathered together at Rabaul from various sources were taken in a Betty aircraft to

134

A VP-11 Black Cat on the Sepik River, New Guinea (Frank W. Morris collection)

the Japanese base at Truk and later transported to Japan, where they sat out the rest of the war. Of the VPB-52 Cat crew that went out that night in November, only Buck Arbuckle survived to tell the story.[4]

Just after midnight on November 25, Hal Sommer, skipper of VPB-52, was prowling an area about 75 miles west of the enemy complex at Rabaul when his radar operator picked up a large force of several ships on his equipment. A few minutes later the wakes of several fast-moving vessels came into view. Sommer picked out one and executed a glide-bombing attack. The entire bomb load was released at about 700 feet and all missed the target. The intended victim, a destroyer, opened up with tracers and fire from its main batteries. Sommer opened to a distance of about 25 miles and proceeded to track the enemy formation. He radioed his position and the situation to Lieutenant Bill Lahodney, who was also searching the Bismarck Sea that night.[5]

Lahodney arrived at the position a short time later and homed in on radar. At about two miles and 1,200 feet, he could make out a large zigzagging wake. It belonged to a cruiser flanked by several destroyers.

135

He pushed the nose of the aircraft over and began a steep dive toward the violently maneuvering target.*

The attack on the big ship was made from port quarter to starboard bow and although the intervalometer was set to provide bomb spacing of 75 feet, it is probable that the weapons hit closer together, due to the steep angle of the dive and the low altitude of the drop. The copilot, Ensign H. M. "Hank" Kalstad, released the stick of bombs on Lahodney's signal and the pullout was made between 100 and 150 feet. They found their marks on the writhing target. The starboard waist gunner looked out to see the large superstructure, masts, and the after turret of a big cruiser flash by. The Cat made a climbing turn and came back for a strafing run despite a withering antiaircraft barrage. As the plane approached its wounded victim, there was a violent explosion from the bowels of the big warship. Lahodney continued the run, dropping a cluster of fragmentation bombs from about 400 feet. As he did so, heavy antiaircraft fire enveloped the Catalina, blew off the tunnel hatch, and ripped through the tail section. Lahodney was suddenly aware that he had lost all aileron and partial elevator control and was losing altitude. Adding full power on one engine and somewhat less on the other, he was able to pick up a faltering wing and thus keep the aircraft in the air. Other enemy ships in the formation now picked up the PBY in their searchlights and were making frantic efforts to shoot it down.

Retiring out of range, the wounded Cat slowly climbed to 6,000 feet, still experiencing severe problems with directional control and maneuvering. Lahodney and his co-pilot wrestled with the problem for some time when, suddenly, dozens of searchlights came on and flashes of light could be seen on the ground below. Only then did they realize that they had strayed over the Japanese stronghold at Rabaul. Luck was with them again, however, and a broken layer of clouds covered their escape. They headed east, passed over the southern end of New Ireland and proceeded out to sea. There they altered course to the southwest and headed for home.

The aircraft was still flying but it was not performing normally. Differential throttle had to be employed on the engines to retain control. Excessive power was necessary to maintain altitude and even so, maximum speed was only about 90 knots. Lahodney ordered all excess gear jettisoned—guns, ammunition, tool boxes, catwalks—everything, as Kalstad later remarked, "that was not riveted to the plane itself."

About 50 miles south of New Ireland they ran into a front with heavy turbulence. With no aileron control, and the elevator cables hanging by a

*Believed to have been the heavy cruiser *Aoba* or another ship of that class.

few strands, they were buffeted about for almost two hours before they emerged on the other side.

The problem now was one of navigation, for they had only a vague idea of the aircraft's position. Finally at daybreak they were able to raise the *Half Moon* on the radio and discovered that they had passed to the west of the tender and were off the southern coast of New Guinea. Reversing course they returned to the coastline and followed it eastward until they came upon the base at Samarai about two hours later. There, they made a deliberately hot landing to prevent the tunnel compartment from taking on too much water, and taxied right up to the ramp. There the aircraft sank in shallow water. It had been an eventful night and Lahodney later received the Navy Cross for his skill and daring.[6]

The performance of Bill Lahodney and his crew was a hard act to follow but there was no scarcity of those who were willing to try. Lieutenant (j.g.) William J. Pattison found a large convoy just south of Kavieng on November 30 and, picking out the largest ship, succeeded in making direct hits with two bombs on the 15,000-ton tanker. The ship with its highly flammable cargo was enveloped in flames. A notation in flight engineer D. R. "Smokey" Strader's log book provides a crew's eye view of the action. "Sank 15,000-ton tanker—what a night! Lamoreaux [second radioman] was shot in leg. 45 holes in plane. Heavy ack-ack."[7] At about

Lieutenant Bill Lahodney's Cat after his mishap at Townsville, Australia. (Captain W. J. Lahodney collection)

137

the same time, Lieutenant Charlie Schauffler and his crew scored hits on two destroyers.

On the night of December 9–10, Lieutenant (j.g.) Rudy Lloyd, an ex-NAP, searched along the east coast of New Ireland until he reached the narrow waist about halfway to Kavieng. There he crossed over the island into the Bismarck Sea and then proceeded northwest along the coast in the bright moonlight. Between Dyaul Island and New Ireland he spotted an 8,000-ton merchantman heading north at slow speed. Lloyd climbed to 1,200 feet and maneuvered so as to make the approach up-moon. When he reached the desired position, he pushed over into a 30-degree dive, picked up 150 knots and released all four bombs manually. Three of them hit the ship and threw considerable debris into the air, although there was no characteristic flash. Lloyd made a quick turn and strafed the ship, pumping tracers directly into the target. By the time he had completed his run, the vessel had already begun to settle by the stern. By the third pass, the stern had gone under and the bow was sticking out of the water at a 60-degree angle. Then it was gone. Through the entire engagement, there had been no antiaircraft fire, no lifeboats or rafts were put over the side, and there was no evidence of survivors.

Lieutenant (j.g.) William M. Flenniken sank a medium-size cargo vessel on the night of December 12–13. The following night Rudy Lloyd found a cruiser anchored in the Steffen Straits about 16 miles southwest of Kavieng. It was a bright moonlit night and as he bore in for his attack, he encountered heavy antiaircraft fire. Lloyd made his run from the port bow to the starboard quarter and released his bombs manually in quick succession from 300 feet. Two of these scored direct hits aft of amidships. Intense antiaircraft fire from shore batteries and the arrival of enemy planes prevented an accurate assessment of the extent of damage inflicted.[8]

On the night of the 18th, Bill Flenniken found a surfaced "I"-class submarine, and sank it. The submarine was observed going down by the stern with a number of survivors in the water. The following night Hal Sommer sank a medium-size cargo ship and strafed another larger one. It was a good night because Lieutenant Alex McInnis also hit a merchant type which, when he departed, could be seen burning from more than 30 miles away. Lieutenant Bob Dilworth scored on a large cargo type on the night of the 23rd. He also strafed and dropped fragmentation bombs on a destroyer in the same convoy.

By the end of the month the squadron had sunk or damaged two cruisers, three destroyers, two submarines, and 76,000 tons of merchant shipping in 137 missions. They had also provided patrol services for the surface bombardment of the Japanese base at Gasmata on November 29,

138

Lieutenant Bill Lahodney (lower right) and his crew. (Captain W. J. Lahodney collection)

and for the invasion of Arawe, about 60 miles east of Cape Gloucester, on the night of December 14.

By the first of January 1944, after six weeks of intensive and successful anti-shipping operations, VPB-52 moved to Port Moresby as part of the rotation schedule which had been established for the Black Cats. They again relieved VPB-11 which had been engaged in air–sea rescue, convoy activities, supply drops, and special assignments. Searches for enemy radar installations (ferret operations) fell in this latter category. On the first of February, Lieutenant Bob Dilworth and his crew were sent to Finschafen at the end of the Huon Peninsula on the northern coast of New Guinea, to operate from the *San Pablo*. Finschafen had been secured by the Allies in October 1943 but Japanese ground forces were not far away and the installation was a handy target for enemy air strikes. The new occupants were still somewhat edgy, and on three occasions while operating from Finschafen, Dilworth's plane was fired upon by friendly ships in the area. The Cat crew discovered the reason for this sensitivity on the 13th, during an enemy air attack in which the *San Pablo* dispatched one of the enemy aircraft with her guns. But despite these diversions, the duty was not particularly exciting for the members of the

Cat crew, compared to their activities in November and December just past. Dilworth found a way to remedy the situation.

On the night of February 11–12, after an uneventful flight during which they were shot at only once by shore batteries at Cape Gloucester, Dilworth decided to look in on the big Japanese air base at Wewak. Approaching from the north with rain squalls at his back, he first spotted lights. Then, as he got closer, he was able to make out the airfield and a cargo vessel moored nearby.

Dilworth climbed to 1,500 feet and flew between layers of clouds until he had almost reached the airfield. Then he dropped down out of the clouds and proceeded across the field at 1,000 feet. To his great surprise he found himself caught up in the landing pattern with enemy planes all around him. They were easy to see because all had their lights on. One was directly ahead of him at a safe interval while another was only a few hundred feet behind. The PBY had cut the Japanese pilot out of the pattern and he was annoyed about it. Pulling alongside he flashed his lights on and off to signal what he thought was one of his own pilots to turn on his lights. He was so close by this time that the waist gunners in the PBY could see his cockpit lights. Dilworth kept going as if he belonged there.

When the Cat reached the edge of the field it did not turn with the other aircraft but nosed over and commenced a run on the ship which was riding at anchor just off the end of the runway. "Let em go!" Dilworth yelled to his copilot, who squeezed the electrical-release pickle switch to drop one bomb. "All of them!" shouted Dilworth, and the copilot got them off in quick succession.[9]

The first bomb hit the Wewak lighthouse and demolished it. The second and third bombs hit the ship. As the Cat made a steep turn to the right, the unfortunate enemy vessel was seen to roll bottom up and begin to sink. It was a fine sight and a worthy effort, but Dilworth was just getting hot. Bringing the plane's machine guns to bear, he proceeded to strafe shore facilities and barges tied up alongside the piers, handling the old Cat as if she were a fighter. By the time the astonished Japanese pilots in the landing pattern realized what had happened, the Black Cat had conducted its business, made its departure, and was swallowed up by the darkness.[10]

From this episode, another Black Cat song was born:

You gotta wewee on Wewak when you
    join COMSOWESTPAC
You gotta wewee on Wewak or Combs
    won't send you back

Morobe's fine, and Madang too, but
   Wewak is the place for you.[11]

And so on. . . .
Bob Dilworth was awarded the Silver Star for his night's work and
became something of a legend in his own time.

11

Courage

Black Cat operations moved ashore in late December 1943. This move coincided with the arrival of Patrol Bombing Squadron 34 to take up the task of search-and-attack missions. It was a soggy introduction to a new environment.

> The day we arrived in New Guinea it was raining. It was raining the day before, too. In fact, it rained every day. Some days it rained twice.[1]

The new advanced base at Samarai was only a few miles east of the mainland and not far from Namoia Bay where the Cats had been operating from the tender *Half Moon*. It boasted a seaplane ramp which enabled the PBYs to be hauled out of the water when necessary, and a nose hangar for maintenance. Except for overhaul, all repairs could be accomplished there.

The operating area was well sheltered from the prevailing winds at that time of year. The seadrome of course was not lighted, so planes normally took off before sundown and landed after sunrise. If a plane had to return to base prematurely due to mechanical malfunction or other emergency, the pilot simply had to do the best he could under the circumstances. A crashboat was always on duty in case of a mishap and also to guide the aircraft to its mooring or to the ramp buoy.

Samarai had once been the capital of British New Guinea and some of the amenities, in the form of government buildings, had survived. The officers were quartered in the old Governor's mansion which, while somewhat picturesque, had seen better days. A wide verandah which completely encircled the house was used as a sleeping area with rows of cots protected by mosquito netting. The house stood on pilings and beneath it there was a shower, of sorts, made from an old five-gallon drum with holes punched in the bottom.[2]

Enlisted men lived in tents, quonset huts, and miscellaneous wooden buildings which had once been used by the colonial government. An old chapel served as the squadron office. Meals for officers and enlisted men were served in a common quonset-type mess hall. While living conditions overall were hardly ideal, Samarai was an improvement compared to other forward areas where Black Cat squadrons had operated.

The skipper of VPB-34 during this period was Lieutenant Commander T. A. "Tom" Christopher, a leader of considerable ability who always seemed to be in the thick of things when there was action at hand. He too was a staunch advocate of masthead-level attacks, which probably accounts for much of his squadron's success.

VP-34 crews began their familiarization flights with VP-52 the day after Christmas and conducted their first independent operations on the 31st. Three aircraft went hunting that night, one flown by Christopher, one by the Executive Officer, Lieutenant Vadm V. "Vad" Utgoff, and a third by the Operations Officer, Lieutenant Ellis Fisher.

Tom Christopher was first out, responding to intelligence information which reported an enemy warship in the Bismarck Sea just north of New Britain, heading toward Cape Hoskins. He found the ship, a two-stack destroyer, at about 2150 and made an immediate attack. Coming in low from the stern, he dropped his stick of bombs, scoring a direct hit with a 500-pounder. There was a large explosive flash, which told the crew they had done their enemy considerable damage. Having expended his bombs, Christopher headed for the Japanese base at Garove Island to try out the quad fifties which had recently been installed in the nose of his aircraft. After raking the installation with gunfire and receiving considerable antiaircraft fire in return, he set a course for home, arriving over Samarai at dawn. It had been a successful first night.[3]

During the time that Tom Christopher and his crew had been making their attacks, Vad Utgoff and Ellis Fisher had struck off to the north across the Bismarck Sea, to search the area around the Admiralty Islands for enemy shipping. Fisher flew clockwise around the islands while Utgoff made his sweep in the opposite direction. At about 0200 on January 1st, Ellis Fisher came upon a 9,000-ton cargo vessel at anchor in Hyane Harbor on the east side of Los Negros Island. It was an easy mark and he sank it with little difficulty, thus claiming the first Japanese ship destroyed in the new year. He topped it off by strafing a smaller ship also

143

Engine maintenance was routinely performed with the craft moored to a buoy. (D. R. Strader collection)

moored there, causing an undetermined amount of damage with his fifties.

VPB-34 had gotten off to a fine start. In the early-morning hours of January 3, however, Lieutenant (j.g.) Roger Means was conducting a raid on Garove Island when his aircraft was badly shot up by ground batteries. Means was killed but his copilot, Lieutenant (j.g.) Bill Lavis took over the controls and managed to bring the damaged Cat home.

The pilots and crews of VPB-34 found that there was considerable

Lieutenant Ellis Fisher (lower left) and his crew made the first kill of the new year. (U.S. Navy)

enemy activity in the assigned operating area. Three or four planes went out every night looking for a fight. One plane would proceed almost due north, arriving just south of New Britain by nightfall. Then it would cross over the enemy-held island in darkness to begin its search on the opposite shore in the Bismarck Sea. Another aircraft headed further east and, when night came, made its way up St. George's Channel past the great enemy base complex at Rabaul. A third Cat flew through the Vitiaz or Dampier Straits to prowl along the northern coast of New Guinea as far as Wewak. Allied ground troops were now pushing northwesterly along the coast of New Guinea and the Japanese used the darkness to resupply and reinforce threatened positions in this area with small barges.[4] These were ideal targets for the quad fifties and they sent many a barge and other small ships to the bottom.

Vad Utgoff went out on January 11 and flew along the New Guinea coastline. Finding no targets, he made two bombing runs on the enemy airfield at Awar. On the second pass six searchlights flicked on and the Cat found itself the center of attention in a hail of antiaircraft fire. In trying to escape the lights, Utgoff maneuvered the aircraft so violently

145

A crash boat sweeps the sealane. PBYs in the background are moored in the buoy patch.
(U.S. Navy)

that he tumbled the attitude gyro. After that inhospitable encounter he proceeded along the coast to Blup Blup Island near the mouth of the Sepik River, where he found a lugger anchored in a small cove. "I made several strafing runs with the fifties but had to turn away too early each time to avoid flying into a mountain."[5] Finally, he approached the target in a steep dive, dropping his last two bombs and using full force on the yoke during the pull-out. It was a tight squeeze and he swore that he smelled the dank vegetation below as he made his recovery. The lugger took a direct hit amidships and quickly sank. On the way home he found a small tanker and made two low and very effective strafing runs with the .50-caliber guns, setting the vessel afire and leaving it burning.

That same night, Lieutenant (j.g.) S. B. Bradley searched the northern part of the Bismarck Sea. At about 0230, the radar operator detected a ship off the western end of New Hanover Island and as they bore in on the contact, another blip appeared nearby. Moments later, both ships came into view about a mile offshore, proceeding at reduced speed. Bradley went for the lead vessel, a two-stack destroyer, making his attack at 300 feet on the starboard quarter. Both ships began firing as the aircraft approached, having concluded that they had been discovered. The Cat penetrated the barrage which the ships threw into the air and dropped all four bombs in a string with the intervalometer set at 40 feet. There were three misses but one bomb, a 1,000-pounder, appears to have bounced off the side, exploding as it sank beneath the ship. The stern of the destroyer lifted several feet out of the water and all antiaircraft fire from that vessel ceased. The other ship continued to shoot at the retreating aircraft and Bradley elected to leave the area without ascertaining the extent of damage done.[6]

The three regular nightly missions were frequently augmented by a fourth aircraft as availability and enemy activity might dictate. The duration of all these missions averaged anywhere from twelve to fifteen hours, although some went seventeen hours and longer. Unlike their amphibious cousins, the PBY-5s had no landing gear and therefore weighed about 2,200 pounds less. This difference meant that each aircraft could carry more pounds of weapons or fuel, and this gave it a better striking capability. All through the night these Cats prowled among the enemy-held islands and poked their lethal noses into coves along the shore in search of prey. As dawn approached they headed for home, timing their departure to be out of the Bismarck Sea by first light. For if they lingered too long they might fall victim to an early-morning flight of Zeros.

Black Cat operating tactics were now becoming all-too-familiar to the Japanese, who tried various methods of counteracting them. At first, the

VP-34 pilots are briefed for a mission. (Rear Admiral T. A. Christopher collection)

147

These enemy ships never reached Rabaul. (Rear Admiral T. A. Christopher collection)

Japanese ships made no attempt to fire on an approaching Black Cat, in the belief that to initiate the shooting only gave away the ship's position. The Japanese knew by this time that the PBYs were equipped with airborne radar, but did not know how accurate that device was. They also reasoned, correctly, that at some point in the final run in, the pilot would have to pick up the target visually if an attack was to be effective.

Due to the phosphorescence of tropical seas, a ship's wake showed clearly in the darkness and was like an arrow pointing directly to the target. Realizing this, some Japanese skippers tried reducing speed or even stopping when an aircraft was heard in the area. But radar would have already given the ship's presence away. When a Cat found a ship hove to and crouching in the darkness like a great hunted beast, it was a slaughter. Without forward movement the ship had no flexibility to maneuver and outsmart the attacker. And the emotion of mercy was unknown to the Black Cats.

Perhaps the most effective defensive tactic the Japanese employed was to hug the shoreline. This often enabled them to blend into the land mass as seen on radar, and worked especially well when there was high ground in the background. Even so, there were open areas to cross and one was never sure when one of these night creatures would come hurtling out of the darkness, bent on vengeance.

The Japanese also tried to catch the low-flying Cats as they penetrated into the Bismarck Sea. They knew, for example, that at least one of the

148

Cats moved up St. George's Channel just after dark. And they knew that it exited the same way just before dawn. To exploit this knowledge, they placed flak ships across this choke point. These were typically small vessels or barges which mounted several machine guns. The idea was to put up a barrage as the Cats passed through in hopes of knocking one down, or at least making their access to the Bismarck Sea more difficult. And the Cats did fly low through this choke point, mostly to get below the severe thunderstorms which seemed to hang over the area continually. But the Cats came to expect these volleys during transit, and even though some aircraft may have been hit by a stray round or two, none were ever shot down as a result of this tactic.

Fighters were also sent up at night in an attempt to stop the carnage at sea, and PBYs were fired upon by these aircraft more than once. But the enemy pilots had no radar and could only grope in the darkness trying to locate these flying apparitions. The Cats, on the other hand, could see with their electronic eyes if enemy aircraft was approaching, and could then dive for the water where they disappeared against the backdrop of the black ocean. And if radar was primitive in those early days, it nevertheless gave the Cats a critical edge in their operations against a courageous but frustrated enemy.

Occasionally an enemy fighter would pick up a Cat visually and make a run on him. "They opened up at such a distance that their fire was inaccurate and the [PBY] would lose them right away by a quick turn right or left and double back on them, scissor with them, and lose them."[7]

On the afternoon of January 15, information reached Samarai that a large enemy convoy from Truk had entered the Bismarck Sea and was headed toward Rabaul. Land-based Army bombers could not make an attack on the convoy before dark. If action was delayed until daylight the next day, however, the formation would have reached the cover of a large front extending along the entire southwest coast of New Ireland. Under cover of weather, the enemy ships would reach Rabaul and unload their cargo, which by this time was sorely needed by the Japanese defenders. It was up to the Black Cats to make the interception.

Tom Christopher and his officers poured over the charts. If the intelligence information was accurate, they should be able to make contact with the enemy at about 0130 off New Hanover Island, just west of the northern end of New Ireland. Six planes, all that could be spared, were readied. Four of these planes were loaded with the customary two 500- and two 1,000-pound bombs. The other two each carried two 500- pounders and one Mark 13 torpedo.

Takeoff time was at 1800 and the six planes headed north. Crossing over into the Bismarck Sea in darkness, they immediately spread out in a loose scouting line to find the enemy convoy. The weather was unusually good that night, with scattered cumulus clouds at about 1,200 feet and a quarter moon providing just the right amount of light.

Tom Christopher made first contact with the enemy at 0108 northwest of New Hanover proceeding on a course of 150 degrees at a speed of 10 knots. As he approached the formation, he could make out four large cargo vessels and two cruisers. About eight miles to the west he could see a second group of ships, consisting of two smaller merchant types and some escort vessels. Having heard the Catalina's approach, the Japanese knew they had been discovered and prepared for the worst. Tom Christopher orbited nearby and called in his other aircraft in order to make a concentrated attack. The enemy, he noted, seemed to have a bad case of nerves. "The cruisers seemed to have great difficulty in keeping the merchantmen in position, and they were milling around in circles, and

Japanese cargo vessel sunk in shallow water by Lieutenant Ellis Fisher and his crew. (U.S. Navy)

150

got all spread out. The other convoy came over and joined them, and the cruisers were just dashing back and forth in among this mess of ships trying to give them adequate coverage.[8]

By about 0230, three of the other PBYs had arrived on the scene. The remaining two aircraft were delayed by distance and weather, and the attack was begun without them. Ellis Fisher moved in first and made a torpedo run on the lead cruiser coming in from the ship's starboard side. Because torpedo attacks are best made from a beam aspect, the target has an opportunity to bring to bear all its guns on one side on the attacking aircraft. And this is exactly what happened in this case, with the second cruiser also pumping out rounds to augment the firepower of the first. Fisher bore on. Positioning himself at about 100 feet off the water at 105 knots, he waited for the right moment and squeezed off the drop. Nothing happened.

Fisher moved out of range and circled around to try again. This time even the merchantmen and another small escort vessel were firing at him but he continued on, getting even closer to the target before he attempted manual release. Again, the torpedo hung up in its mounts. By this time, the cruisers had the picture. The Cat was after them. They appeared to forget about their slow-moving charges in the convoy and concentrated their efforts on saving themselves. Again, the Cat dove, levelled off at 100 feet and zeroed in on one of the big warships. For the third time, the obstinate weapon refused to drop. A serious oil leak had now developed in the starboard engine. Reluctantly, Ellis Fisher and his crew departed the area and headed for home.

But the fun was just beginning. S. B. Bradley who had been orbiting about six miles from the formation, now made his move. Climbing to 3,500 feet, he moved in close, using a broken layer of clouds to mask his approach. When he was almost on top of the enemy ships, he nosed over in an unusually steep dive of perhaps 70 degrees. As he broke through the clouds, he found himself about a mile from a fat tanker which he immediately chose as his target. Flattening his dive angle to about 50 degrees, he came in fast (for a PBY), indicating about 200 knots. Antiaircraft fire was now intense but Bradley concentrated on his chosen victim as the Cat plummeted toward the water. At 150 feet, he pulled out and pressed the intervalometer bomb-release switch for a stick of four. The mechanism failed to function. Fortunately, the copilot pulled the starboard emergency-release handle at the same time, releasing one 500- and one 1,000-pound bomb from under the starboard wing. Both were direct hits amidships. Bradley maneuvered violently to escape the antiaircraft fire which enveloped him and retired to safe distance where he observed his handiwork with some satisfaction.

151

Tom Christopher later described the sight. The ship was a large tanker loaded with gasoline. When Bradley's bombs found their marks "she went up into a beautiful torch. In the light of that the other planes picked out their targets. . . ."[9]

Next to try his luck was Lieutenant (j.g.) Loring M. Bates, Jr. He moved in on a freighter approaching from the starboard side at an altitude of 500 feet. When he was only a few hundred yards from the target, he pushed over into a dive and let all four bombs go in a stick at 125 feet. There were no hits and the Cat made its escape at a low altitude, skimming a few feet off the water.

At about this time, Vad Utgoff came upon the scene and, in the light of the fire from the burning tanker, he began a torpedo run toward a group of ships which included one of the cruisers. The enemy could hear the Cat coming but apparently thought it was another bombing attack and concentrated his gunfire skyward. Utgoff slipped in underneath and launched his fish. It was a perfect textbook run, 125 feet, 105 knots at drop point. Distance was about one-half mile with plenty of running time for the weapon to arm. The torpedo left the aircraft on cue—but there was no explosion and the enemy ships steamed on. Utgoff still had two bombs left and he was determined to make them count.

By this time the convoy was fast approaching a line squall which the enemy ships clearly intended to use for cover. Christopher decided to make his attack before that could happen. Moving in at 500 feet, he chose a large cargo vessel. He lined up his approach from port bow to starboard quarter and when he was almost on top of the vessel, Christopher dove on the target. As the Cat bore in at close quarters, the bow gunner sprayed the deck with his twin thirties, silencing one gun on the ship's stern. Releasing all four bombs on the intervalometer, Christopher concentrated on making good his escape. It was a good drop—right on the money, but there was no explosive flash. Suddenly, there was a blast which threw Cat crewmen into the bilges. Seconds later, a plume of water, smoke and debris rose 200 feet in the air over the stricken vessel. All fire from the target ship had now ceased but guns from the other ships in the convoy zeroed in on the fleeing aircraft. There seemed to be a wall of tracers ahead. If they could not go through that hail of bullets, perhaps they could go under it. Christopher dove for the water to make good his withdrawal.

Now it was Vad Utgoff's turn to try again. He had seen the spectacular explosion aboard Christopher's target ship and chose another large cargo vessel nearby. Utgoff began his attack about a mile from the target, diving quickly from 1,200 to 200 feet in an attempt to get under the antiaircraft fire coming at the airplane from all directions. It was from all kinds of guns both heavy and light and it followed the aircraft in its dive. Utgoff released both 500-pounders together as he made his run from port quarter to starboard bow. One hit the ship's side and exploded, shooting a bolt of fire outward and parallel to the water. The other appeared to have gone through the deck plates and went off. As the aircraft made a circling escape, fire was seen amidships and below decks in the forward part of the ship.[10]

It was a beautiful sight. Three large vessels whose cargoes would never reach the Japanese garrison at Rabaul were burning brightly below. With weapons expended, the four remaining planes headed for Samarai and a good day's sleep. At 1045 the next morning, an Army reconnaissance aircraft arrived at the scene of the battle to survey the damage. There they found one of the ships in its final stages of agony and watched it go under. The other two were burning, and belching smoke and debris from periodic explosions from within. Soon they too would be claimed by the sea. There was no sign of life except for a few empty lifeboats and the flotsam and jetsam of battle. The Black Cats had done their job well.

Three nights later on the 18th, the Cats were at it again. Ellis Fisher swept the area between New Hanover and the Admiralties. Then, in a careful search of Manus and Los Negros Islands, he made contact with a 2,500-ton tanker entering a narrow passage near the town of Papitalai at the eastern end of Seeadler Harbor. He dove on the target which fired back at the plane as it made its attack. Fisher dropped one 500-pound bomb which hit the vessel amidships. All firing ceased, the ship stopped dead in the water and took on a noticeable port list. Fisher circled and made another attack, this time missing the target by about twenty feet. But there was no need for further attacks. The vessel settled quickly in the shallow water and when the plane left the area only the mast could be seen. Tom Christopher and Lieutenant Jules M. Busker each sank a cargo ship that night. Vad Utgoff, who was searching for a submarine between Garove Island and New Britain, played "hide-and-go-seek" with a Japanese night fighter. He found the sub and initiated an attack but the wily enemy skipper detected his approach and submerged before Utgoff could make his drop.

On the night of the 22nd, Lieutenant Harold L. Dennison found a destroyer near Wewak and made a bombing run. All the bombs missed, which infuriated Dennison. He turned on the enemy vessel and engaged it in a gunfire duel, quad fifties against all the guns of a full-size destroyer. Tom Christopher recalled the incident some time later. "He made about three passes on this destroyer with his .50-calibers and he must have shot him up pretty badly, because he got them all over the ship and he saw a couple of small fires started that were eventually extin-

153

guished. At the same time he had that old Cat so damned riddled it was a wonder he got home."[11] Christopher himself attacked another destroyer that same night but the results of the attack could not be determined.

Lieutenant James F. "Jim" Merritt, Jr. attacked and sank an 8,000-ton transport on the 27th, and that same night Lieutenant Nathan G. Gordon (of whom we shall hear more later) damaged a destroyer. Christopher attacked a small cargo vessel with his quad fifties on the night of February 5. His plane was badly shot up and one of his crewmen wounded. Gordon sank three large and eight medium-size barges, and damaged a number of others by strafing on February 8, but Tom Christopher topped this when he destroyed thirty barges with his quad fifties the following night. Ellis Fisher destroyed a tanker, a small submarine, and five boats on the 13th, and teamed up with Harold Dennison and Lieutenant Ross Vandever on the night of the 15th to nail a large cargo vessel. To the enemy skippers whose misfortune it was to sail the Bismarck Sea during that period, it must have seemed that there was no respite and no place to hide. The Cats even flew up rivers and attacked vessels at their moorings.

Just when the Black Cats of VPB-34 were getting warmed up, it was time to give up the search-and-attack mission to VPB-33, and move on to air-sea rescue duties at Port Moresby. The progress of the war and the advance of Allied forces along the northern coast of New Guinea meant that the action was moving farther west. Air strikes were being made almost daily and Fifth Air Force Headquarters, which controlled air-sea rescue activities, were moved up to Nadzab, just inland from Lae. Part of the squadron was sent forward to Langemak Bay at Finschafen to operate from the tender *San Pablo* and later from the *Half Moon*.

The procedure for rescue operations called for one or more Cats to orbit near the target while a daylight air strike was in progress, waiting for a call. When it came, the Cat would proceed to the site, land in the water, and pick up the crew. A grid system was used to simplify the problem and if a plane had to ditch, the pilot would broadcast his grid position. Sometimes there was fighter coverage for the rescue operation and sometimes not. Frequently, disabled aircraft found it necessary to ditch close to shore and it then became a contest between the Cat and the Japanese to see who could get there first.

One such mission performed by a VPB-34 aircraft was especially notable. It was flown by Lieutenant Nathan Gordon and his crew on February 15. Gordon's Cat, sometimes known as "the *Arkansas Traveller*" in deference to the pilot's home state, was assigned to cover a large B-25 raid against the enemy base at Kavieng on New Ireland. The fighting had been particularly heavy that day and the PBY went directly

154

Medal of Honor winner Lieutenant Nathan Gordon.
(U.S. Navy)

to the scene of action, looking for airmen in the water. The Cat crew could see that the Army aircraft had done their job well, as smoke billowed from the burning Japanese base.

A raft was spotted just offshore and although there was no sign of life in the vicinity, Gordon knew that a human head bobbing in the water can be easily missed from the air. He went down to investigate.

The heavy swells off the beach were not conducive to a smooth landing and the Cat hit hard. Water came in around the seams and drained into the bilges but the old PBY stayed afloat. They taxied around the raft to make sure there were no survivors, then lifted back into the air in a well-executed open-sea takeoff.

No sooner was the Cat airborne when they were called by a B-25 circling nearby. The pilot of that aircraft had spotted another raft with men aboard close to shore. The Japanese had put a boat over in an attempt to capture the Americans but the B-25 roared down over the surf and discouraged that line of approach with its guns. The enemy now contented himself with firing at the raft and its occupants from the beach.

Once again, the Catalina landed in the heavy swells and taxied over to the raft. The Japanese gunners now shifted their attention to the aircraft. It was evident that the B-25 crewmen could not be hauled aboard the moving aircraft so Gordon pulled the mixture controls back and the props ground to a stop. The raft came alongside and the men were quickly hauled aboard. With slugs sprinkling the water around them, the two pilots started the engines and the Cat labored through the swells and bounced into the air.

Now Gordon received another call—more men in the water. He located the three crewmen quickly, landed, and once more cut his engines. Again, he was taken under fire by the enemy shore positions and again he made it back into the air. With nineteen people aboard, including his own crew, Gordon headed for home. But before he got very far, the B-25 pilot was on the air again. He found still another raft with six more men aboard.

Already overloaded with people and a large volume of water sloshing around in the bilges, the young pilot knew this would be a squeaker. Yet he could not leave six Americans to fall into the hands of the Japanese. Returning to Kavieng, he found the raft only a few hundred yards offshore. Because of the direction of the wind and swells, Gordon was obliged to make his approach over the beach and through a hail of gunfire. Setting the big Cat down in the water, he pulled up to the raft and shut down the engines. Six lucky crewmen were hauled aboard, the engines came to life and the badly leaking Cat began its takeoff run. The Japanese threw everything they had at the plane to prevent its escape. The black hull plowed through the swells, the engines straining to heave the waterlogged Cat from the water. Gradually, the airspeed increased and after what seemed an eternity, they were airborne.

For the last time, the battered old Cat headed for Finschafen. Gordon put crewmen to work with buckets to get rid of some of the water in the bilges and thus lighten the load. Hours later, they splashed down in Langemak Bay and transferred fifteen grateful airmen, some of whom were badly injured, to the field hospital.

Admiral Halsey was especially impressed with the performance of Gordon and his men, so much so, that he took time to dash off a message of congratulations. "Please pass my admiration to that saga-writing Kavieng Cat crew. X-ray. Halsey." Nathan Gordon was later rewarded with the Congressional Medal of Honor for his day's work.[12]

Going for the Jugular

By the end of February, the once-formidable enemy stronghold at Rabaul had been bombed to rubble and effectively neutralized. Shipping to and from Simpson Harbor had been reduced to a trickle of small cargo ships and barge traffic which travelled at great peril. The Black Cats of VPB-33 based at Samarai found the hunting in this area very disappointing. The squadron CO, Commander R. C. "Bob" Bengston, found a small merchantman on the night of February 15 and another on March 9, and sank both of them. Lieutenant Commander Fernald P. "Flip" Anderson came upon a large number of enemy barges stealing along the northern coast of New Guinea west of Finschafen on March 14, and destroyed twenty-five of them by strafing. For the most part, however, enemy seaborne traffic in the Bismarck Sea had dried up.

There was no need at this point to mount a major effort to capture Rabaul. What remained of Japanese forces there offered no threat to the Allied advance and were simply allowed to wither on the vine. The same fate was to befall Kavieng on New Ireland.

The Allies continued westward. Lieutenant Jim Merritt landed six U.S. Army infantrymen on Los Negros Island in the Admiralties in the early-morning hours of February 27 to reconnoiter enemy positions for the imminent invasion. The following afternoon, Lieutenant Walter O. Pierce landed off the enemy-held island in broad daylight, picked up the recon team and brought them safely home with their first-hand information.

Allied forces landed in the Admiralty Islands on February 29. Not long afterward, the Black Cats of VPB-33 and VPB-52 began operating from Seeadler Harbor, the tenders *Tangier* and *San Pablo* providing their support. Ground fighting was still underway on the islands and the Senior Officer Present Afloat (SOPA) issued a written order forbidding anyone to go ashore except on official business. Shore-based naval personnel were not permitted to leave their work enclaves or their quarters. "At night," the order warned, "anyone above ground is shot at—no questions asked."[1] The enemy ashore tried to knock the Cats out of the sky on landing approaches and snipers took pot shots at the Cat crews as they serviced the planes at their moorings. The SOPA Order concluded with a terse reminder which no one really needed: "Keep alert and remain alive."[2]

There was no time for tourism in any case. The Cats flew searches as far north as the big enemy base at Truk, and during the last week in March made four consecutive strikes on the enemy airfield at Woleai in the Carolines. Flip Anderson flew the last of these raids on March 31, making a dive-bombing attack from 8,000 feet only hours before a large carrier strike on the atoll. On April 5, Anderson made a similar attack on Wakde Island off northwestern New Guinea. It was the first of a series of air raids on that enemy base, leading to an invasion. Anderson's attack started several large fires, one of which was still burning intensely five hours later.

During this period, VPB-34 engaged primarily in rescue missions flying from Langemak Bay at Finschafen. Most of these were in enemy-held territory. Tom Christopher picked up fourteen wounded Marines on March 9, after a late evening open-sea landing at Talasea, New Britain, and a night takeoff. Two nights later, he landed near Wakeo Island off the northern coast of New Guinea to rescue five survivors of an engagement at Hansa Bay on March 6 in which their PT boat had been sunk.

On April 25, Lieutenant Jules Busker took off from Seeadler Harbor on a daylight mission to look for the crew of an Army aircraft which had ditched in the open sea somewhere between the Admiralties and Truk. The men had been missing for five days and it was a big piece of ocean. The prospect of their rescue was very slim. Nevertheless the Cat crew gave it their best shot.

As Busker's plane flew over the vast ocean expanse, it happened upon a PBY from another squadron on the water and flew over to investigate. The other Cat had located the Army crewmen and had made an open-sea landing to pick them up. The survivors' life raft was at the Cat's side. But as the VPB-34 aircraft made a low pass, the men on the water could be seen signalling it to land. The PBY had apparently run afoul of a heavy swell, torn open its hull, and was sinking fast.

A VP-33 Black Cat being hoisted aboard the tender for repairs. (George Favorite collection)

Busker made his approach carefully to a full-stall landing and touched down without incurring any damage. "We lucked out," says Busker of his landing. "The ole girl was shipshape with only one rivet popped in her hull."[3]

The new rescue team quickly taxied over to the stricken Cat. By this time, her crew and the survivors of the Army aircraft had taken to life rafts and all that was visible of the PBY was her fast-disappearing tail. Minutes later, it too had slipped beneath the waves. Fifteen men were hauled aboard Busker's Cat, one of them badly injured and others also in need of medical attention. Now, with a total of twenty-nine people aboard, the trick was to outsmart the swell system and get back into the air without suffering the fate of the other PBY.

Busker drained off a thousand gallons of fuel before making his move. He instructed his copilot, Lieutenant (j.g.) William G. "Bill" Syring, to "hold the throttles at full bore" on takeoff.[4] Then turning into the wind, they began their run.

We started by riding up and down the swells and reached near flying speed when our last water contact threw us violently into the air, whereupon Bill Syring actually bent the throttles in the forward position. Although we nearly stalled back in, our trusty Cat stayed aloft and I knew we had it made.[5]

159

Open-sea landings were hazardous under the best conditions. (Captain J. M. Busker collection)

The Allied offensive was moving rapidly now and General MacArthur had his sights set on an invasion of Mindanao by mid-November. In pursuit of this objective, which had the blessing of the Joint Chiefs of Staff, he pressed toward the westernmost end of New Guinea, whence he would seize a jumping-off point to the Philippines. Bypassing the Japanese base at Wewak, he landed his forces at Aitape, Hollandia, and Tanahmera Bay on April 22. A few weeks later the Cats, always in the forefront, were operating from Hollandia, supported by the tenders *San Pablo* and *Orca*.

Further westward along the coast lay Wakde Island. This enemy base which boasted an excellent airfield, was invaded by MacArthur's forces on May 18. On May 27, the Allies went ashore on Biak, a large island about one hundred and seventy miles west of Wakde and by the end of July, Sansapor on the extreme western end of New Guinea was also occupied. Now, MacArthur had only one more stop to make before making his move into the Philippines.

On July 9, Frank Wagner, now Rear Admiral, relieved Commodore Combs as Commander Aircraft Seventh Fleet. A few days earlier, veteran Cat pilot Captain Carrol B. "Doc" Jones had taken over as Commander, Fleet Air Wing 17.[6] Jones had already made a name for himself as CO of VP-43 in the Aleutians. There, during the "Kiska Blitz" of June 1942, he and his squadron mates had transformed their PBYs into dive bombers, screaming down through a thick Aleutian overcast to hit enemy ships and shore installations at Kiska Harbor. Jones well understood the extraordinary versatility of the unassuming PBY.

Frank Wagner, of course, had commanded PATWING 10 in the black days of 1941 and 1942 when the Japanese seemed to be "unstoppable." This time, the shoe was on the other foot and it seemed almost poetic justice that Wagner should take command as his planes moved back into familiar territory. That he remembered well the painful retreat through the Netherlands East Indies was perhaps reflected in a covering memorandum to instructions which he issued not long after his arrival, in which he tried to impart some of the hard-learned realities of combat against the Japanese. "It must be remembered by all pilots," he said, "that instructions, methods, and techniques are valueless unless the Black Cat pilots and crews are inspired by an all-compelling desire to destroy the enemy. Be aggressive as well as painstaking in search, be bold as well as skillful in attack and success will be yours."[7] He and the Cat crews were in complete accord.

Lieutenant Commander Vad Utgoff had relieved Tom Christopher as CO of VPB-34 on May 12. Since the middle of February, the squadron had been engaged primarily in air–sea rescue activities, saving a total of seventy-seven men by July 17. At that time VPB-34 was shifted back to its search-and-attack role, operating from the seaplane tender *Orca* anchored in the lagoon at Woendi Island, just off the southeast tip of Biak. The Cats flew their missions westward into the Molucca Sea as far as Celebes Island, looking for targets.

Vadm Victorovich Utgoff, known affectionately as the "Mad Russian," had grown up with airplanes. His father, a Russian Count, had flown in the first Curtiss seaplanes to be acquired by the Imperial Russian Navy in the early 1900s. Later, fleeing to the United States after the Russian Revolution, the Utgoffs settled on Long Island, New York. A friend of the family and fellow *émigré*, named Igor Sikorsky, constructed his first American-built airplane in Vad Utgoff's back yard.

The young CO was tall and slender, and, not surprisingly, carried the look of a bonafide aristocrat. The impression was accentuated by his use of a six-inch cigarette holder, of the same type used by President Roosevelt. Utgoff was hard-working, colorful, and popular and had a keen sense of humor, which is readily apparent in his series of articles called "The Cat's Tale," published in 1946.[8]

This tour of search-and-attack missions started, unfortunately, on a sour note. On the night of July 23, Lieutenant (j.g.) Richard W. Ball sent a contact report to base, advising that he had found a target in Kaoe Bay at enemy-held Halmahera Island and was commencing an attack. Base radio heard nothing more from Ball's aircraft but another Cat operating

161

in the area received weak and garbled transmissions from this plane as much as an hour and fifteen minutes later. Then all transmissions ceased. The plane did not return to base.

The cruel business of war continued. On the 30th, Lieutenant (j.g.) Joe Ball (not related) searched the area south of Ceram looking for targets, but found only a few small enemy vessels. After several strafing runs, his radar operator picked up a large merchant vessel which Ball promptly attacked and hit with all four bombs. When he departed the area, only a frothing bubbling circle remained. The following night, the squadron Executive Officer, Lieutenant Norman L. "Norm" Paxton, found three enemy ships hiding in a cove on the north coast of Mangole Island and placed two bombs squarely on the superstructure of a large cargo vessel, starting several fires. Antiaircraft fire from this ship, an 8,000-ton freighter, and its escorts was heavy. One shell exploded in the leading edge of the starboard wing, severing the aileron cable and holing the wing panels, the strut, and the propeller on the starboard engine. Despite

Soggy but safe. Airmen from a downed B-25 are rescued in the open sea by Lieutenant George Favorite and crew of VP-33. (George Favorite collection)

this damage, the faithful Cat brought Paxton and company all the way back to Woendi without further incident.

Vad Utgoff found a destroyer escort northeast of Boeroe Island on the night of August 1. One of his bombs exploded against the port side, all the way aft. The blast lifted the stern of the vessel clear of the water and displaced it sideways. A cloud of black smoke was emitted from the ship's stack and she began circling uncontrollably to port. And that was the way the Cat left her.

On the 4th, Norm Paxton sank a small tanker and Lieutenant (j.g.) Darwin "Dar" Day got a 300-ton cargo vessel. For the most part, however, the hunting from Woendi had been less than satisfactory. The primary reason for this was that there were no targets close by. The Philippines to the northwest were still slightly beyond reach, and the nearest worthwhile targets could only be found by flying six or seven hundred miles to the west. This meant that there was very little chance to search the area and make an attack before it was time to head for home.

On August 6, VPB-34 was joined at Woendi by planes of VPB-11 under Lieutenant Commander Thomas S. White. His squadron had just returned to the forward area from western Australia but its pilots and crews were no strangers to this kind of operation. In fact, they had served longer in the Black Cat business than any other unit. Nevertheless, it was a dangerous game for even the most experienced hands and a week after VPB-11's arrival at Woendi, a PBY was lost. Lieutenant Thomas S. Ragsdale and his crew, ten men in all, did not return from a search-and-attack mission on the night of August 13-14. They had been prowling the Molucca Passage between Halmahera and Celebes Islands when their last radio report was received.

The two squadrons were soon moved to a more forward position to get maximum use of their long-range capabilities. On August 22, the Cats left Woendi and joined the tenders *Orca* and *Half Moon* at Middelburg Island near Sansapor. The distance to enemy ports and shipping lanes in the Molucca Sea was greatly reduced by this move and the hunting improved. There was no sheltered harbor or bay at Middelburg, however, and the tenders simply set up operations in the lee of the island. For the Cats, each takeoff and landing was an adventure in itself.

The new forward position now brought even the Philippines within range of the Black Cats. In fact, the Cats were now the only long-range assets which could make it all the way, perform their mission, and still have enough fuel to make it back to base. On the night following their arrival at Middelburg, Vad Utgoff and Norm Paxton of VPB-34 flew two Cats north to the Davao Gulf area of Mindanao. They were the first PBYs to fly over the Philippines since the daring night flight from Corregidor in

163

1942. They detected a number of enemy planes in the air but were not attacked. The Cats made runs on several ships but were hampered in their attacks by poor visibility. There were lights on the ground, brightly burning. The Japanese still felt secure in the Philippines—but the night flight of the Black Cats on August 22 was a harbinger of things to come. For the enemy, time was running out.

Meanwhile, the hunting to the west picked up, particularly in the vicinity of the Japanese base at Manado on the northeastern end of Celebes Island. Vad Utgoff found a freighter there on August 26 and served up a direct hit amidships. That same night Lieutenant (j.g.) Melvin Essary, also of VPB-34, sank a small tanker off the town of Manado. Two nights later, Joe Ball bombed a large freighter in Manado Bay and left it listing sharply. Ball's aircraft received heavy antiaircraft fire from the ship as well as from shore batteries, but managed to make good his escape without serious damage.

On the night of August 29, Lieutenant (j.g.) William L. "Willie" Garrett Jr. had a field day. Searching in Manado Bay, he first came upon a concentration of small craft into which he dropped one 500-pound bomb. Not far away he sighted a small stack-aft-type vessel and hit it with another 500-pounder squarely amidships. The ship blew up and sank. Next, he dropped two 100-pound general-purpose bombs in the center of a group of nested barges. Then he hit a barracks building ashore with two small fragmentation bombs and strafed a two-masted schooner with his .50-caliber machine guns. Still looking for trouble, he flew along the coast toward the town of Manado where he found several small ships anchored. Choosing one which lay no more than a hundred yards offshore, he made a diving approach over the town and dropped his last 500-pounder at 170 knots and 100 feet altitude. The bomb exploded under the vessel and she disintegrated in a shower of debris. With all weapons expended and a feeling of considerable satisfaction, Willie Garrett and his crew headed for home.

Norm Paxton got a hit on August 30 and Vad Utgoff damaged and probably sank a small stack-aft vessel on the 31st. This ended VPB-34's search-and-attack tour for the time being and the squadron returned to Manus Island in the Admiralties.

Meanwhile, veteran VPB-11 had also gotten in some good licks. Lieutenant Nelly Nelson, who had sunk the destroyer *Mochizuki* in Jacquinot Bay during October of the previous year, found another one in Lembeh Strait off Celebes Island on August 29. He dove through intense antiaircraft fire from ships and shore batteries to severely damage the enemy warship. Tom White, the squadron CO, sank a small cargo ship in nearby Bangka Strait and another in Manado Harbor on the 30th. And if this were not enough, the scores got even better in September.

They blazed a trail of burning ships from the Solomons to the Philippines. (U.S. Navy)

On September 3, Lieutenant Tom Hine made a flight into Davao Gulf, where he found a 7,500-ton tanker. Fire from gunner Howard R. "Trigger" Kenyon's .50-caliber gun was extremely accurate that night, and finding the vulnerable spots he quickly dispatched the vessel. Kenyon describes the incident like this:

About midnight we found this ship in a little cove in the lower Philippines. The pilot bombed twice and missed and in the meantime the Japs hit us in the wing with 7.7 machine gun fire. I then opened up with the .50-caliber and set them on fire. When we left, the flames were 1,000 feet in the air.[9]

Lieutenant Jack Penfold sank three small ships and damaged two others the following night in Sarangani Bay at the southernmost end of

165

Mindanao. On the eighth, Lieutenant (j.g.) James D. "Jim" Dyer also ventured into the Philippines to sink a 10,000-ton tanker off Basilan Island, just south of Zamboanga.

General MacArthur now needed one more steppingstone before he could invade the Philippines. He chose Morotai, just north of Halmahera Island. From there he planned to operate his land-based bombers against Mindanao.

The landing at Morotai on September 15 was uneventful, but it soon became apparent that the partly completed Japanese airstrip there was unusable and that a new U.S.-built field could not be completed until early October. But a seaplane carries its own airfield on its bottom and the Black Cats moved up from Middelburg Island immediately. By September 19, they were in full swing, operating from tenders at Morotai. Again they would be the cutting edge, first to carry the unwelcome message to the Japanese in the Philippines, now only 300 miles away: "MacArthur is coming."

At about this time, VPB-101* under Lieutenant Commander L. E. "Steve" Johnson arrived on the scene and joined the other Cats in their forays.

Now it is necessary to backtrack a few weeks to pick up VPB-33, which completed a period of air–sea rescue work in late August and moved forward to Middelburg Island, ready to give the Japanese a taste of their own brand of hell. Flip Anderson had relieved Bob Bengston as Commanding Officer of VP-33 on May 28, 1944. Anderson, a very capable officer of Swedish descent, was a tenacious warrior who achieved considerable success not only by the number of ships which he personally sank, but as an effective leader when the big push was on.

The Black Cats of VPB-33 began their record-breaking tour on September 1, 1944, operating from the tender *Orca* off Middelburg Island. During the first four nights, they sank nine ships and damaged several others, including a destroyer. An enemy seaplane, a number of barges, luggers, and other small craft were also sent to the bottom by strafing. Then, on the night of the 5th, Flip Anderson and his crew took off for the big Japanese base on Zamboanga on the southwestern end of Mindanao. This was the first Allied plane to attack in the vicinity of that enemy stronghold. The Japanese were clearly not expecting this kind of company so soon. After a long flight northward across the Celebes Sea, the Cat arrived off Zamboanga and began looking for suitable targets. Almost immediately, Anderson came upon two destroyer escorts nested

*On October 1, 1944, VP-101 flying Catalinas, had its squadron designation changed to VPB-29. The other half of the squadron, then flying PB4Y-1 aircraft, retained the number 101.

Lieutenant Commander Flip Anderson got two destroyer escorts at Zamboanga (Captain F. P. Anderson collection)

together about three miles east of the town. The Japanese had not yet discovered the Catalina in their midst. If they heard the drone of the engines they assumed it was one of their own planes. The Americans had not penetrated this far into the Japanese-occupied area before.

Anderson made a wide arc to position himself north of the two unsuspecting targets. Then, when the setup looked just right, he pushed the nose over and pounced! Two bombs fell from masthead height. Each struck one of the ships with a resounding blast and both vessels exploded. Flames shot into the air almost a thousand feet and the fires were still visible forty miles away as the Cat trimphantly wended its way home.[10]

The carnage continued during the first half of September. On the night of the 16th, Lieutenant Jim Merritt, who had transferred from VPB-34 to become the Executive Officer of VPB-33, found a 7,500-ton freighter in Kendari Harbor on the southeast end of Celebes Island. Merritt placed two 500-pounders on the target during the first run. He was not sure, however, that the damage to the ship was sufficient to finish her and made several strafing runs. This airplane was not equipped with the .50-caliber installation in the nose and the results were inconclusive. Merritt had one 500-pound and one 100-pound bomb left, and decided to use these to make it an undisputed kill. This time he would get so low that he could not miss.

167

This Cat sent an enemy cargo ship to the bottom—under protest. (Captain F. P. Anderson collection)

That was a close one. Lieutenant C. B. Sillers examines a bullet hole in his windshield.

Down he went, aiming the Cat between the two masts to get a good drop. But he was lower than he thought on this run and as the Cat passed over the ship, the starboard wing struck a forward King post and broke it off. The plane shuddered from the impact, but the wing held. The 500-pounder had released as planned split seconds before and hit the ship, but the 100-pound bomb hung up and did not drop. Now all he had left were small fragmentation bombs which were carried inside the aircraft. He decided to use them to finish the job.

On the next run, Merritt dropped six parafrags, one of which fell in an open hold, exploded, and started a fire. Men could be seen on deck running about and trying to extinguish it but the Cat put a stop to that with its machine guns. Finally, when the vessel had become an inferno, Merritt adjudged the job complete and they set a course for Middelburg Island. Arriving at the tender, they were amazed to discover that they had brought home with them a piece of the ship's King post imbedded in the leading edge of the wing. It was a fine souvenir![11]

Ten days later Lieutenant Merritt received the following letter from Doc Jones:

UNITED STATES FLEET
FLEET AIR WING SEVENTEEN

A 16-3(0-cn)
Serial: 545   27 Sep 1944
From: The Commander Fleet Air Wing SEVENTEEN
To: Lieutenant James F. MERRITT, (A-VN), USN
Via: The Commanding Officer, Patrol Bombing Squadron
          Thirty Three

Subject: Ramming Tactics Plane versus Surface Ship—Disapproval of.

1. The history of naval warfare is replete with incidents of ramming as an effective method of destroying opposing ships. Students of history will recall such battles as Salamis, Actium, Lepanto and Lissa wherein ramming was the primary method of sinking. Formidable pointed rams were provided by the naval constructors of those days on the underwater part of the bow. Even in modern times, underwater rams were built into the bows of battle ships with the expectancy that ramming tactics might be employed. However except for antisubmarine tactics, ramming has not been effectively employed since the days of our own Civil War. Even in the times of Nelson and J. P. Jones ramming tactics assumed a secondary role in ship to ship contact, the placing of a ship alongside an enemy for the purpose of boarding being preferred.

169

2. A cursory comparison of the construction of aircraft and surface ships will readily reveal that in a case of contact between the two, the plane will come out second best because of its lighter construction. Furthermore, a careful inspection will reveal the complete absence of a ram device on aircraft.

3. In consideration of the foregoing, that part of your action on the night of 16-17 September 1944, wherein you deliberately rammed the ship you were attacking, is disapproved. It is considered that factors contributing to the destruction of the ship can be assessed as follows: bombs, 98%, machine gun fire 2%, and ramming 0%.

4. The official report covering your action has not yet been received but it is assumed that being so imbued with naval tradition you issued the proper commands to our gallant crew when the decision to ram was made and that your boarding party was properly equipped and indoctrinated.

5. It is entirely possible, due to shortage of critical materials in the Japanese Empire, that Japanese surface ships may eventually be lightly enough constructed to make ramming tactics by aircraft profitable. At such time your experience may prove invaluable in the indoctrination and training of crews in these revolutionary tactics.

C. B. Jones

Copy to
ComAir 7th Flt
CFAW-10

On the night of September 23, Lieutenant (j.g.) William B. "Wild Bill" Sumpter made three spectacular kills in one run. Searching the Davao Gulf on Mindanao, he discovered a large 10,000-ton *Chitose*-class seaplane carrier. Two destroyer excorts were refueling from the larger vessel, one on each side. It was a Black Cat's dream come true. Sumpter came in on the three helpless vessels at masthead level, releasing four bombs in a stick. The first struck a destroyer escort, the next two hit the tender, and the fourth exploded below decks in the other destroyer escort, causing three secondary blasts which threw the plane 200 feet in the air. Both escort vessels sank almost immediately. Sumpter then swung around and raked the tender with his guns. She was on fire and listing to one side, and the Cat pilot was determined to finish her off. After several strafing passes, the big ship rolled over on her side and settled in the water. Scratch three![12]

VPB-33 lost a man that night when Lieutenant (j.g.) Robert W.

Wild Bill Sumpter dropped his entire bomb load on an enemy cruiser at Toli Toli Bay, F. P. Anderson collection) Celebes Island (Captain

Schuetz bombed a 10,000-ton transport at Toli Toli Bay, Celebes Island. As the Cat made its run on the ship, heavy gunfire hit the starboard propeller, blew two cylinders off the engine, and holed the wing. Schuetz hung on grimly and dropped his string of bombs, two of which struck the side of the big ship. As the plane passed overhead, however, gunfire ripped through the bottom, fatally wounding the navigator, Ensign LeRoy Flatau. The plane was shaking violently but Schuetz was able to climb to 2,000 feet where he shut down the gasping engine and feathered the prop. Ordering all unnecessary gear jettisoned, he flew the badly damaged Cat back to the tender, a distance of 550 miles on one engine. As Flip Anderson later pointed out, "we had no alternate bases to which we could return! It was the home tender or else!"[13]

That same night, in Kolono Bay, Celebes Island Anderson hit a 10,500-ton tanker which caught fire, rolled over and sank. A gunner on another Cat operating in the same area was wounded during an attack which damaged a small freighter.

VPB-33 flew its last flights of this search-and-attack tour on the night of October 3–4. Lieutenant (j.g.) John Zubler's aircraft was badly damaged, one crewman was killed and two others wounded during an attack on a 3,000-ton freighter. Zubler got off all his bombs, two of which hit the vessel amidships, but the cost had been high.

Wild Bill Sumpter was also out that last night. He and his crews had already sunk thirteen ships and damaged three others during the month of September and were looking for something to cap off their score. They found it in the northwest part of Celebes Island in Toli Toli Bay. That night the weather was clear as they flew along the coast with a large bright moon lighting their way. As they passed the entrance to the bay, they took a look inside and much to their surprise found two cruisers, a destroyer, and a destroyer escort lying at anchor there. All were darkened but the moon clearly illuminated them. Sumpter played it cool. Assuming that he had also been seen by the Japanese, he continued on past the mouth of the bay and then headed out to sea. There was no indication from the enemy ships that the Cat had been detected.

About an hour later, Sumpter turned around and headed back. He radioed base advising them of his find and his intention to attack at 0100. If nothing was heard from the Cat thereafter, the people back at the tender would not have to guess what happened.

As they bore in on Toli Toli Bay, the pilot briefed his crew. They were going to make landfall some distance up the coast and skirt along the shore in an effort to mask their approach by the mountainous terrain. At the last minute, they would burst into the bay and hopefully catch the Japanese ships by surprise. No one was to open fire with the machine guns until Sumpter gave the word.

Everything went as planned until the final moments. The Cat approached from behind a hill at a thousand feet and Sumpter pushed the nose over about a mile and a half from one of the cruisers. But by this time they had been seen and when they were about a quarter of a mile from the drop, all four warships opened with heavy and light antiaircraft fire. It was like a thick wall which no airplane could possibly penetrate. Sumpter later observed that he could have lit a cigarette on the tracers—they were that close. Still, he held the Cat in its dive and continued his attack run down the centerline of the target ship.* At 125 feet of altitude, he let go with his entire bomb load—no spacing. All of them landed on the unfortunate victim. The blast enveloped the aircraft and Sumpter thought they had been hit. But the aircraft still seemed to respond to his command. He dove for the water and headed for the entrance to the bay. Tracers and heavy gunfire continued to burst around the Cat as it

*Believed to have been a *Katori*-class cruiser.

172

skimmed the surface. Moments later it made a sharp turn, almost dipping a wing tip in the water, and ducked behind a point of land.

Checking the Cat over, Sumpter determined that it had not sustained any serious damage. He took up a position in the darkness just outside the bay and orbited while watching fires burn aboard the enemy vessel. Then, with weapons expended, he began the long flight back to the tender.[14]

Wild Bill Sumpter's spectacular pyrotechnic display was the icing on the cake for VPB-33. In fact, all the pilots and crewmen of that squadron had performed magnificently to amass a record of enemy tonnage sunk, destroyed, and damaged that no other Cat squadron was able to surpass. In the course of just over one month, forty-three ships totaling 103,500 tons had been sent to the bottom or otherwise destroyed. Twenty more adding up to 53,500 tons were severely damaged. A large number of miscellaneous vessels of various descriptions were also dispatched, although their tonnage is not included in the 157,000-ton total documented for this squadron during this period.

General MacArthur in a dispatch to the Seventh Fleet Commander Admiral Kinkaid praised the "recent magnificent performance" of the Black Cats. "No command in the war," he said, "has excelled the brilliance of their operations."[15]

13

Battle Scars

On September 15, 1944, the day that General MacArthur's troops went ashore at Morotai, Admiral Nimitz's Marines landed on Pelelieu in the Palaus, less than 500 miles east of Mindanao. While MacArthur had been moving swiftly along the southern route toward his objective, Nimitz had driven across the Central Pacific, and in June his Fifth Fleet under Admiral Spruance routed the Japanese Navy in the Battle of the Philippine Sea. By August, this entire area, including Guam and the northern Marianas, was under effective U.S. control. The time for the invasion of the Philippines was near.

The Joint Chiefs of Staff envisioned a landing by MacArthur at Sarangani Bay on Mindanao by mid-November, and another landing on Leyte to the north by December 20. But Admiral Halsey, whose Third Fleet had made air strikes against Mindanao on September 9 and 10, believed that Mindanao should be bypassed and that MacArthur should go ashore at Leyte instead. Carrier-based air power would support the landings and eliminate the need to seize airfields on Mindanao for the same purpose.

Both Nimitz and MacArthur liked the idea and on the day of the Morotai and Pelelieu landings, the Joint Chiefs of Staff approved the essential elements of Halsey's plan. MacArthur would invade the Philippines at Leyte on October 20, 1944.

Meanwhile, the Black Cats continued their nightly forays from Morotai. For the Japanese in the Philippines who were digging in for the inevitable invasion, these nocturnal visitors must have seemed like ghosts from the past, returned to haunt them. On the night of September

174

20, Lieutenant (j.g.) Donald L. Hand of VPB-11 penetrated all the way to Ormoc on Leyte, where he attacked a freighter and left it foundering on a reef.

MacArthur left nothing to chance in his planning. He was in contact with Filipino guerrillas on Leyte and had the word spread to coastal inhabitants to evacuate the area where the softening-up bombardment was to take place. He sent Commander Charles Parsons and Lieutenant Colonel Frank Rouelle to Leyte to coordinate the operation with Filipino guerrilla leader Colonel Ruperto K. Kangleon. Lieutenant Walt Shinn of VPB-11 was assigned the mission of getting Parsons and Rouelle there safely. His Black Cat put them ashore south of Tacloban, capital of Leyte Province, without incident on October 12, eight days before the invasion. The landings at Leyte proceeded according to plan, and on the afternoon of October 20 MacArthur himself, accompanied by Philippine President Osmena, waded ashore.

Back at Manus Island in the Admiralties, Patrol Bombing Squadrons 33 and 34 had been engaged in training and upkeep and some rehabilitation leave in Sydney, Australia. There, it is said, they befriended many of our Australian allies, particularly the female variety, and consumed large quantities of a potent alcoholic concoction called "turkey-wurkey." Now they were called back to action and by the 23rd, five planes from each of the two squadrons had arrived at Leyte and began operating from the tenders *San Carlos* and *Half Moon*. They were just in time for some major fireworks. Japanese naval forces were already steaming toward Leyte Gulf for a major engagement.

The tenders had found a well-sheltered mooring area in Hinunangan Bay off the western side of Cabugan Chico Island. There each of the ships received its detachment of PBYs, five from VPB-34 under the command of squadron commander Vad Utgoff, and another five under VPB-33 Executive Officer Jim Merritt. Soon all ten aircraft were tied up in the buoy patch set out by the ships.

Early the next morning, the *Half Moon* and its moored aircraft were rudely attacked by two single-engine Val type dive bombers.* These were engaged by four F6F Hellcat fighters which happened to be in the area. One of the Japanese planes was shot down and the other escaped. That afternoon, there was a meeting aboard the *Half Moon* attended by Utgoff, Merritt, and the Task Unit Commander Jack I. Bandy, who was also CO of the *Half Moon*. During the conference, the ship was again assaulted, this time by two twin engine Sallys.** One made a bombing run on the ship while the other went after aircraft on the water. Both

*Type 99 Aichi carrier-based dive bombers
**Type 97 Mitsubishi twin-engine heavy bombers

A VP-33 Cat makes its buoy. (George Favorite collection)

bombing runs were unsuccessful, although one bomb hit just short of the ship, bounced over the stern, and landed in the water on the other side without exploding. One crewman was wounded by strafing and the *Half Moon*'s gunners sent one of the planes away smoking.

With the lengthening of the day came word of the approaching Japanese fleet. At dusk, some of the Cats were dispatched to the south into the Mindanao Sea, to locate the enemy. In the meantime, powerful Allied surface forces were preparing to meet the Japanese as they en-

176

tered Leyte Gulf through Surigao Strait. Earlier in the day, the *San Carlos* had weighed anchor and moved north to San Pedro Bay. Sometime after the planes had departed on their search missions, the *Half Moon* also got under way, leaving the remaining aircraft with crews aboard at their buoys, and moved a few miles north to anchor on the west side of Cabugan Grande Island. But the ship had not moved far enough from the imminent surface engagement and it soon became apparent that it had positioned itself on the sidelines between the two opposing fleets. Jack Bandy decided to move further north.

Before the *Half Moon* could depart the area, the Battle of the Surigao Straits began with a great outpouring of thunder and fire from heavy guns. It was a spectacular sight and the little tender had a ringside seat. Squadron personnel and ships company alike lined the rails to watch the display.

Meanwhile, the Cats which were in the air had scoured the area south of Surigao Strait but failed to locate the enemy. Jim Merritt's radar had gone down shortly after takeoff and his technicians worked feverishly to get it back on the line. On the way out they spotted a surface force visually, but decided it was too close in to be the enemy and proceeded further south, still working on the stubborn radar set. In retrospect, Merritt now believes that he may have passed over units of the approaching Japanese fleet without realizing it. After a fruitless search of the Mindanao Sea, the Cat headed home, arriving sometime before dawn. There Merritt found a battle raging, and his aircraft was taken under fire by both Japanese and Allied ships. Merritt instinctively dove for the deck and flew inland behind some hills that gave him protection. But the ground suddenly rose ahead of him, whereupon he added full power, hauled back on the yoke, and skimmed over the tree tops reaching out to pluck the Cat from the sky. After what seemed like a very long time, he made radio contact with friendly forces who cleared him to land. It was well that they did, for he was almost out of gas.[1]

Lieutenant (j.g.) Maurice W. Moskaluk, also of VPB-33, was not so fortunate. He too returned to Leyte Gulf and was met by a hail of antiaircraft fire from American guns. His Cat was shot up so badly that when he finally landed, it sank almost immediately. The crew was picked up by a crash boat and no one was hurt.

If Leyte Gulf was hazardous for the Cats, it was disastrous for the Japanese. Vice Admiral Shoji Nishimura's force of two battleships, one cruiser, and four destroyers, was first attacked by PT boats as it approached Surigao Strait, then by destroyers as it entered the Gulf, and finally by the heavy guns by the Allied cruisers and battleships. The admiral went down with the battleship *Yamashiro* and in the end only one of his ships, a destroyer, escaped. Vice Admiral Kiyohide Shima, with three cruisers and four destroyers, followed Nishimura into Leyte Gulf and fared somewhat better, but was still badly mauled by the superior Allied force awaiting him there. By daylight, what was left of the attacking Japanese force was in full retreat.

The action now shifted to the east of Samar where a more powerful enemy force under Vice Admiral Takeo Kurita was headed south toward Leyte Gulf. This force was engaged and held at bay by a task group of escort carriers and destroyers under Rear Admiral Thomas L. Sprague. Sometime after noon on the 25th, the Japanese fleet retired to the north.

That evening, Vad Utgoff took off and headed north along the east coast of Samar in search of Admiral Kurita's retreating fleet. At dusk he spotted a life raft and one man. But his assigned mission was to find Kurita. The radioman got off a message to base, reporting the raft's position and requesting that a rescue vessel be dispatched to pick up its lone occupant. The Cat continued on its search to the north. By the time the PBY reached the San Bernadino Strait, however, the Japanese force had already passed through.

Utgoff and his crew headed home and at first light spotted the man in

A VP-44 Black Cat detachment at Mangaldan Airfield, Lingayen Gulf, has breakfast guests. (Captain G. Bogart collection)

the raft they had seen the night before. The Cat had burned off most of its fuel during the night and was now at a good weight to attempt a landing.

The big seaplane eased down to check the surface. Heavy swells were running and there was very little wind. As the plane commander put the aircraft down gingerly, it hit the crest of one of the swells hard and tore open the bow. The plane bounced back into the air and Utgoff poured on the power in an attempt to stay airborne. The Cat clawed the air but she had lost too much airspeed and began to settle back onto the water. One wing dropped, the float dug into another swell, and the whole plane did a partial 180-degree turn before coming to a sudden stop. The battered Cat took on water quickly and began to go down by the nose. No one was seriously injured and before the aircraft sank, the Cat crew was able to launch a raft and pile in.

They picked up the man in the small raft, a pilot from one of the escort carriers which had engaged the Japanese in that area the previous day. Then they paddled the cumbersome rubber boat all the rest of that morning until about 1230, when they rounded the southernmost tip of Samar. There natives spotted them and paddled out in their canoes to escort the Americans to their village. About this time a TBF torpedo bomber happened on the scene and provided cover until the ragtag fleet made it to shore. It was well that it did, for an enemy plane was attracted by the activity and had to be driven off. The entire group of Americans was picked up that afternoon by another VPB-34 Cat, which landed in a sheltered area near the village to make the final rescue.[2]

Control of the air in the vicinity of Leyte Gulf was still a matter of dispute. Enemy planes attacked ships anchored there with regularity. This was no small problem for the PBYs, which were often mistaken for attacking Japanese aircraft. Consequently, the ground rules for Black Cat operations went something like this: "Take off before dusk but do not return to land before dawn." No one had to explain why. There were too many gunners with sensitive trigger fingers who had learned from bitter experience that it was better to shoot first and ask questions later.

Lieutenant Lawrence R. "Larry" Heron headed the top-secret electronic-countermeasures "Ferret" group, whose job it was to detect, evaluate, and fix enemy radar stations. The Ferrets used Black Cat aircraft and were ostensibly part of their operations, but had specialized responsibilities and reporting requirements. One night, Heron took off on a reconnaissance flight and headed up San Fernando Strait between Leyte and Samar. Suddenly the starboard engine caught fire and the tender was notified that the Cat was returning for an emergency landing. By this time it was dark and Heron elected to land on the far side of the Gulf to avoid being fired on by the ships. But nobody had told the commanders

179

of the Army antiaircraft batteries ashore. The result was predictable. "We got the hell shot out of us," Heron recalls.[3]

Landing some distance away from the tender, the Cat pilot had a difficult time finding his buoy. To make matters worse, smoke had been laid among the ships to conceal them. Although lights were taboo, Heron finally decided to use the aldis lamp to find out where they were. "Put that goddamn light out," someone bellowed from one of the ships. "Don't you know there's an air raid?" "We know," responded one of the crewmen aboard the Cat, "We're it!"[4] Then they moved out of the area quickly lest one of the gunners took offense. Such was life at Leyte Gulf at that stage of the war.

On October 29, a typhoon bore down on the area with winds exceeding 70 knots. Taxi crews were put aboard the PBYs at their moorings and when the storm hit they attempted to ride it out. Some cast off from their buoys, since these can be dragged by an aircraft in high winds. These Cats then headed into the wind and tried to hold their positions with the engines, using the buoys as reference points with near-zero visibility. The reference was critical, for without it the pilot could no longer tell whether he was moving forward or drifting backward. Ultimately, he could expect to be blown ashore, or worse, to collide with another aircraft.

To make matters worse, a seaplane is difficult to maneuver in high winds. The aerodynamic design which enables it to fly will also cause a plane to weathercock (head into the wind) like a weather vane. In very high wind it is virtually impossible to turn the aircraft around. Any attempt to force it to turn all the way out of the wind with an engine may drive first a wing-tip float, and then the wing itself, under water. If it becomes absolutely essential to reverse direction, the only course of action available to the pilot is to turn out of the wind a few degrees and sail the aircraft backward. A form of tacking is also possible using this technique, and many a boat pilot has made his buoy in this manner.

To a seaplane pilot, a knowledge of seamanship is almost as important as being able to handle the aircraft in the air. In this case, on October 29, 1944, the seamanship was superb and most of the aircraft survived. Two of the Cats were driven ashore and damaged. Two PBYs of VPB-33 were on night searches, and took refuge at Palau until the typhoon passed.

During the next few months, the Cats were employed not only to search for the enemy, but to conduct rescue operations as well. One of the most spectacular rescues ever made by these aircraft took place in Ormoc Bay on the western side of Leyte during daylight hours of December 4.

The Ormoc Bay area was Japanese-held territory and on the night of December 3–4, the *Cooper* had been torpedoed and sunk there in a surface action with the enemy. The ship had been blown in two, but half the crew had survived. Some had swum ashore to take their chances on being captured by the Japanese. But many had chosen to remain in the water, in hope of rescue by the Catalinas. Five planes from VPB-34 and one Army OA-10A were dispatched to the area to pick up survivors. The Army also provided fighter cover for the operation.

Joe Ball set his Cat down in Ormoc Bay and began picking up clumps of survivors. Two enemy destroyer escorts had been carefully camouflaged with jungle vegetation and could not be easily seen from the air as they nestled against the shore. But Ball spotted them as he taxied about. Making no sign that he had seen the enemy destroyers, he continued to haul men from the water. The Japanese apparently thought that their camouflage hid them from the Catalina, and with U.S. Army fighters circling overhead elected not to give away their position. Joe Ball picked up fifty-six survivors before he made his departure. Including his crew there were sixty-three people aboard when he turned into the wind and pushed the throttles forward. The plane required a three-mile run before it could get off the water.

Melvin Essary rescued forty-five men that day while Dar Day picked up twenty-five more. The two other VPB-34 aircraft found nine men in one case and sixteen in the other, and the Army OA-10A also hauled several survivors aboard. In all, it was a spectacularly successful rescue operation.

On December 10, Vad Utgoff flew north to Luzon to rescue some downed aviators on Bondoc Peninsula and some escaped prisoners of war, all of whom had been taken in by Filipino villagers. This was deep in Japanese-held territory and eight Marine Corps F4U Corsair fighters accompanied the Cat in case there was trouble. Utgoff landed offshore and took the aviators and escaped POWs aboard. As the Cat prepared to take off with its passengers, word came that a Japanese motor launch was approaching. This was no problem for Utgoff and his passengers because they could make their getaway long before the enemy arrived. But the Filipinos were in a bad spot. They well knew the penalty for having aided and sheltered Americans and had good reason for concern.

Once airborne, Utgoff called the F4Us and apprised them of the situation on the ground. The Marines were sympathetic to the natives' plight and welcomed the chance to do them a good turn. By this time the launch was approaching the village. The Japanese had observed the PBY's departure and it was not difficult to guess what had transpired before their arrival. It would not be pleasant for the villagers. But, one by one, the Corsairs screamed down from the bright tropical sky. The unwary Japanese on the launch never knew what hit them.[5]

It was now time for the Allies to move north again and on the night of

Not since David and his slingshot. . . . (U.S. Navy)

December 14–15, the Black Cats searched ahead of the invasion force bound for Mindoro. Troops went ashore on the morning of the 15th and Army engineers began work almost immediately on an airfield which would support landings on Luzon. This later invasion came at Lingayen Gulf on January 9, and the following day the Black Cats of VPB-71 were ordered to move up there and operate from the tenders *Currituck* and *Barataria*. This squadron of PBY-5A amphibians had recently come up from Morotai where it had been engaged in search-and-attack missions since November 24. Now the Cats fanned out into the South China Sea prowling north to Formosa, the Pescadores, and the coast of China.

For the Japanese, the end was drawing ever closer. The noose had been tightened to the point where the outer defensive perimeter was now drawn from the Bonin Islands through Formosa to Shanghai and thence to southern Korea. The Philippines had been virtually written off, and Japanese defenders there could look forward only to delaying actions and ultimate defeat. The enemy plan was to hold the outer line as long as possible and gird for the final decisive action—the defense of Japan itself. The world did not yet know of a new weapon then in the making which would soon change the face of warfare—the atomic bomb.

To most people such weapons were still in the realm of science fiction in January 1945. In the western Pacific it was Halsey's Third Fleet which carried the fighting closer and closer to the beleaguered enemy. Moving aggressively, as was his style, Halsey launched strikes on Japanese positions on the Asian mainland from Saigon to Hong Kong, and against the enemy stronghold at Formosa.

During the month of February the Black Cats of VPB-71 also prowled the South China Sea, where they sank eight ships and damaged nine others. At that time they moved back to Leyte Gulf and continued their operations from the seaplane base at Jinamoc Island. By now, only VPB-71 and Lieutenant Larry Heron's Ferret Group were operating in the area.* A few other Cat squadrons contributed detachments. In the meantime, VPB-11 had departed for home in November, VPB-34 left in December, and VPB-33 headed east in February.

*   *   *

While there would be more fighting before an Allied victory in the Pacific, the enemy was entering the final agonizing throes of defeat. Much of her once-great merchant fleet now lay at the bottom of the ocean, and the remnants of the Imperial Japanese Navy had taken refuge in well-defended harbors to lick their wounds and prepare for the bitter ending certain to come. The flow of oil, so essential to the continued operation of the war machine, had slowed drastically and the incoming supply of other critical resources was in much the same condition. The Black Cats and their anti-shipping campaign had done much to help place the Japanese squarely on the threshold of disaster.

The PBYs had amassed an impressive record of kills against a competent and powerful foe. That record was especially spectacular because it

*Heron's Ferrets remained in the area flying missions along the Chinese coast until May 1945. VPB-71 stayed on through the war's end.

had been accomplished with machines already past their prime when war began. By 1945, the faithful old Catalinas could reasonably be classified as obsolete. In the beginning, they were all we had. Now that the wheels of production were in high gear, the Cats were being replaced by bigger, faster, better-protected, and more powerful aircraft like the Martin PBM Mariners and the Consolidated PB4Y-1 Liberators.

Slowly, during the last months of 1944 and into the first months of 1945, the Black Cats began wending their way home across the Pacific. They were a sorry sight, dented and pockmarked, with black paint peeling from their battered hulls. Some wore crude patches and others still carried bullet holes that had not yet been plugged. But these were warriors' scars, earned in battle and worn with dignity. And justly so. Never in history has an aircraft so ill-designed for combat wreaked so much havoc on such a dangerous and merciless adversary. Not since David and his slingshot had men gone forth with more courage than those who flew out into the darkness at 95 knots, in search of Japanese Goliaths!

Acknowledgements

Following the trail of the Black Cats has been a fascinating experience. Perhaps the most rewarding aspect has been the opportunity to meet and correspond with many of the people who were directly or indirectly involved in the development of the concept and in the unique operations which ensued. This book would not have been possible without their assistance.

Mr. Ward Holme Tanzer who, in 1944, produced and directed the classic U.S. Navy documentary film *The Story of the Black Cats* provided a wealth of research material collected in connection with that endeavor. Rear Admiral William P. Schroeder, USN (Ret.) furnished an excellent overview of the operations of VP-11 during 1942 and opened up several avenues of additional information. Mrs. Warren S. Pittman generously made available the personal papers of Rear Admiral Clarence O. Taff, USN (Ret.), now deceased, who commanded the first official Black Cat squadron at Guadalcanal. Rear Admiral William O. Gallery, USN (Ret.) skipper of the seaplane tender *Half Moon* and Commander Task Group 73.1 in the New Guinea area contributed an extensive collection of message traffic relating to Black Cat operations. He also provided information on some of the early initiatives taken to develop effective attack capabilities and an insight into the command relationships in the Southwest Pacific area.

Personal interviews with five Black Cat squadron commanders and telephone interviews with a sixth produced valuable information on the operations of individual squadrons and an insight into the personalities of the men who called the shots. For these first-hand accounts I am indebted to:

Captain Fernald P. "Flip" Anderson, USN (Ret.) C.O. VP-33
Captain G. S. "Gerry" Bogart, USN (Ret.) C.O. VP-44
Rear Admiral Thomas A. Christopher, USN (Ret.) originally of VP-21, later VP-101 and finally C.O. of VP-34.
Rear Admiral James O. Cobb, USN (Ret.) originally of VP-11 and later C.O. of VP-91.
Capt. Carl W. Schoenweiss, USN (Ret.) C.O. of VP-54.
Capt. Vadm V. Utgoff, USN (Ret.) C.O. of VP-34.

Details of some of the more spectacular Black Cat operations were provided by Captain William J. Lahodney, USN (Ret.), Commander James Merritt, USN (Ret.) and Mr. William "Wild Bill" Sumpter.

So many people provided material and otherwise aided in the preparation of this book that it is not possible to acknowledge all of their individual contributions in the space allotted. Nevertheless, I would like to extend my deep appreciation to the following persons for their generous assistance:

Commander J. Marshall Arbuckle, USN (Ret.),
Dr. William J. Armstrong,
Mr. William A. Barker,
Ms. Carrie M. Bryant,
Commander Hulon R. Blakeney, USN (Ret.),
Captain Jules M. Busker, USNR (Ret.),
Commander Jack G. Churchill, USN (Ret.),
Mr. Joseph B. Deodati,
Captain D. G. Donaho, USN, (Ret.),
Captain Robert Eslinger, USN (Ret.),
Lt. Commander George U. Favorite, USNR (Ret.),
Captain Ellis J. Fisher, USN (Ret.),
Captain E. F. Hann, Jr., USNR (Ret.),
Captain Donald H. Hartvig, USNR (Ret.),
Captain Lawrence R. Heron, Sr., USN (Ret.),
Commander Charles P. Hibberd, USNR (Ret.),
Mr. Ewing W. Hix,
Miss Julia Agnes Hunt,
Mr. Leonard C. Hylton,
Mr. John D. Jubb,
Mr. Howard R. Kenyon,
Miss Jane E. Knott,

Lt. Charles F. Lewis, USN (Ret.),
Mr. Ken MacWhinney,
Commander Joe McCabe, USN (Ret.),
Mr. Lawrence J. McMackin,
Mr. Frank W. Morris,
Mr. Charles Muckenthaler,
Mr. George F. Poulos,
Mrs. Laura B. Pryce,
Commander Douglas H. Roberts, USN (Ret.),
Mr. Arthur D. Ronimus,
Commander Allan Rothenberg, USN (Ret.),
Aviation Machinists Mate Chief D. R. Strader, USN (Ret.),
Captain Ronald F. Stultz, USN (Ret.),
Lt. Commander John E. Sullivan, USNR (Ret.),
Mr. William B. Sumpter,
Mr. Clarke Van Vleet,
Commander Charles F. Willis, USN (Ret.),
Captain Dave Walkinshaw, USN (Ret.),
Mr. John Zubler.

Notes

Chapter 1

1. See discussion of Taussig testimony in *The New York Times*, April 23, 1940, pp. 1, 8, "Sees U.S. Involved in Far East War"; April 24, 1940, p. 6, "Senators Speed Bigger Navy Bill"; April 25, 1940, p. 7, "Taussig's Statement Denounced by Clark."

2. Letter from the Commander Patrol Wing 2 to the Chief of Naval Operations of January 16, 1941—Subject: Patrol Wing 2—Readiness of.

3. Commander Patrol Wing 2 letter of January 16, 1941.

4. Patrick N. L. Bellinger, unpublished memoirs, held by Naval Historical Center, Washington Navy Yard, Washington, D.C., p. 305.

5. Attack on Pearl Harbor, U.S. Navy Court of Inquiry, Findings of Fact, pp. 1-32.

6. U.S. Navy Court of Inquiry, pp. 1-34.

7. Report of the Commander Task Group 9 (Commander Patrol Wing 2) to the Commander-in-Chief, United States Pacific Fleet of December 20, 1941—Subject: Operations on December 7, 1941.

8. Bellinger memoirs, p. 318.

9. Bellinger memoirs, p. 320.

10. Undated letter from Commander Charles P. Hibberd, USN (Ret.).

11. Hibberd letter.

Chapter 2

1. Recollections of Lieutenant (j.g.) Earl D. Payne, USN, formerly Chief Aviation Pilot, VP-101. Undated.

2. Report of the Commander Patrol Squadron 101 to the Commander Patrol Wing 10 of December 31, 1941—Subject: Bombing attack on Japanese Battleship on December 10, 1941; report.

3. Commander Fleet Air, West Coast to Director of Naval Intelligence of December 12, 1944—Subject: Information Concerning Naval Campaign in Orient, 1941-1942. Enclosure (5) Rough Draft of PatWing 10 Operations, p. 20.

4. Action report of Lieutenant J. J. Hyland, USN, to the Commander Patrol Squadron 101 of January 3, 1942. Subject: Report of Bombing Raid on Island of Jolo.

5. Action report of Lieutenant (j.g.) T. E. L. McCabe, USN, to the Commander Patrol

Squadron 101 of January 3, 1942. Subject: Report of Bombing Raid on Island of Jolo.

6. Action report of Commanding Officer Patrol Plan 101-P-9 to Commander in Chief, U.S. Asiatic Fleet. Subject: Dawn Bombing Attack of Jolo, Sulu, P.I., December 27, 1941—report of. (Christman report)

7. Action report of Commanding Officer, Patrol Plan 101-P-6 to Commander Patrol Wing 10. Subject: Bombing attack at Jolo, Sulu, December 27, 1941 and subsequent incidents, report of. (Dawley report) January 29, 1942. Also see supplementary report—Dawley.

8. Dawley report.

9. Christman report.

Chapter 3

1. Action report of Ensign J. L. Grayson, USNR, to the Commander U.S. Naval Forces, Southwest Pacific, Subject: Bombing Mission; report of, February 8, 1942.

2. Action report of Ensign J. F. Davis A(V)N, USNR, to the Commander in Chief, U.S. Asiatic Fleet. Subject: Encounter between PBY-5 and Jap fighter. January 27, 1942.

3. Letter from Captain D. G. Donaho, USN (Ret.) dated 9 January 1981.

4. Donaho letter.

5. Donaho letter.

6. Action report of Lieutenant Thomas H. Moorer, USN, to Commander U.S. Naval Forces, Southwest Pacific. Subject: Account of action engaged in by crew of PBY-5 airplane number 18 during period February 19 to 23, 1942, dated February 23, 1942.

7. Extracts PatWing 10 War Diary December 7, 1941–May 2, 1942.

8. Gridiron Flight—Narrative Report of Flight from Australia to Manila Bay and Return. Lieutenant (j.g.) Thomas F. Pollock, USN. Undated.

Chapter 4

1. Memorandum from Commander Patrol Wing 2 to Commander-in-Chief, U.S. Pacific Fleet dated May 23, 1942.

2. Letter from Commander Charles P. Hibberd, USN (Ret.). Undated.

3. Interview with Commander Alan Rothenberg, USN (Ret.), February 6, 1980.

4. Rowland, Buford and Boyd, William B., *U.S. Navy Bureau of Ordnance in World War II* (Bureau of Ordnance, Department of the Navy, Washington, D.C.), p. 121.

5. Hibberd letter.

6. Hibberd letter.

7. Hibberd letter.

8. 3rd Endorsement on Lieutenant W. L. Richards, USN, action report of June 18, 1942. CinCPac File No. A16-3/MDY/(90) Serial 01926 dated July 2, 1942.

Chapter 5

1. Interview with Rear Admiral James O. Cobb, USN (Ret.), of November 11, 1980.

2. Cobb interview, November 11, 1980.

3. Toshikazu Ohmae, "The Battle of Savo Island," U.S. Naval Institute *Proceedings* (December 1957), p. 1268.

4. Interview of Lieutenant Commander J. O. Cobb, USN, in the Bureau of Aeronautics, April 26, 1943.

5. Rothenberg interview, February 6, 1980.

6. Letter from George F. Poulos dated January 16, 1981 with narrative of his experiences in VP-11, pp. 16-17.

7. Cobb interview, November 11, 1980.

Chapter 6

1. Cobb interview of November 11, 1980.

2. Cobb interview of November 11, 1980.

3. Samuel Eliot Morison, *History of United States Naval Operations in World War II; The Struggle for Guadalcanal*, (Boston: Little, Brown and Company, 1949), p. 187.
4. Poulos letter of January 16, 1981.
5. Letter from Joe Deodati describing the attack on Tonelei Harbor, Bougainville. Received February 1981.
6. Interview with Charles F. Willis of March 2, 1981.
7. Interview with Ewing W. Hix, November 1980.
8. William F. Halsey and J. Bryan III, *Admiral Halsey's Story* (New York: McGraw-Hill, 1947), p. 121.

Chapter 7

1. Letter from Captain Ronald F. Stultz, USN (Ret.), undated.
2. Moreno J. Caparrelli, "The Black Cats of the Southwest Pacific," *Flying Aces* (July 1944), pp. 45, 55.
3. Henry Ledoux, diary of his experiences in the South Pacific. Published as part of a VP-12 cruise book entitled *Black Cat Command*, ed. Anderson F. Hewitt, (New York, undated).
4. Stultz letter.
5. Stultz letter.
6. Stultz letter.
7. Ledoux diary.
8. *The Old Black Cats*, United States Pacific Fleet, South Pacific Force, Intelligence Division, June 29, 1942, p. 3.
9. Stultz letter.
10. Ledoux diary.
11. Ledoux diary.
12. Presidential Unit Citation to Patrol Squadron 12 for the period November 24, 1942 to June 1, 1943. Signed James Forrestal, Secretary of the Navy, for the President of the United States.

Chapter 8

1. Howard D. Miner, excerpt from VP-54 Drinking Song, unpublished.
2. Interview with Captain Carl W. Schowenweiss, USN (Ret.), November 17, 1980.
3. Schoenweiss interview.
4. Report of Combined Action Against Japanese Surface Combatants (Tokyo Express), VP-54, July 15, 1943.
5. Interview with Commander Douglas H. Roberts, USN (Ret.), February 27, 1981.
6. Roberts interview, February 27, 1981.
7. Letter from Commander Jack G. Churchill, USN (Ret.) of February 19, 1981.
8. Churchill letter of February 19, 1981.
9. VP-54 Description and Analysis of Operations in the Solomon Islands Area, March 11 to December 1, 1943, Night Combat Operations, War Diary Extract, p. 34.
10. Chronological File, VP-Squadrons, Naval Aviation History Office, Bldg 146, Washington Navy Yard, Washington, D.C. Also see "Black Cats," *Flying*, October 1944, pp. 302, 304, 306.
11. Gerard S. Bogart, *The Black Cats of Green Island.* Unpublished manuscript.
12. Patrol Squadron 44 Aircraft Action Report #5, Date of Action August 28, 1944.

Chapter 9

1. Letter from Captain Donald H. Hartvig, USNR (Ret.), dated October 18, 1980.
2. Catalina Operations by Task Force 73 in the New Guinea–Bismarck Archipelago area from August through November 1943. Aircraft, Southwest Pacific Force, (Task Force 73) Air Combat Information.
3. Letter from Howard R. Kenyon, undated.
4. Letter from Lieutenant Commander John E. Sullivan, USNR (Ret.), dated Febru-

ary 1, 1981. Also see Patrol Squadron 11 War Diary entry October 24, 1943.

5. Sullivan letter of February 1, 1981.
6. Letter from Frank W. Morris dated December 9, 1980.
7. Patrol Squadron 11 War Diary for October 1943.
8. Patrol Squadron 11 War Diary for November 1943.

Chapter 10

1. Combat Record of Patrol Squadron 11, Navy Department Release dated December 30, 1944, p. 1. Also see *Patrol Squadron Eleven*, #24 in a series of short sketches of squadrons in World War II. Based on reports field with Aviation History and Research, DCNO (Air).

2. Letter from the Commander Patrol Squadron 52 to the Chief of the Bureau of Aeronautics, dated January 31, 1944. Subject: Installation of four fixed fifty-caliber machine guns in the bow of PBY aircraft.

3. Interview with Captain W. J. Lahodney, USN (Ret.) of March 27, 1981.
4. Interview with Commander J. Marshall Arbuckle, USN (Ret.) of April 5, 1981.
5. Patrol Squadron 52 Aircraft Action Report, date of action November 25–26, 1943.
6. Lahodney interview of March 27, 1981. Also see Report of Action Against an Enemy Cruiser by Ensign H. M. Kalstad (undated).

7. Personal Flight Log of Flight Engineer D. R. Strader, November 30, 1943.
8. Patrol Squadron 52 War Diary December 1 to December 31, 1943 dated Janaury 1, 1944. See entry for December 13, 1943.

9. Charles A. Rawlings, "I Heard the Black Cats Singing," *The Saturday Evening Post*, December 2, 1944, pp. 12-13, 58, 61.

10. Patrol Squadron 52 Aircraft Action Report, Date of Action February 11–12, 1944.

11. Rawlings, "I Heard the Black Cats Singing."

Chapter 11

1. Vadm V. Utgoff and Darwin Day, "The Cat's Tale (Part Six)," *Shipmate*, June 1946, p. 6.

2. Interview with Rear Admiral T. A. Christopher, USN (Ret.) of November 17, 1980.

3. Christopher interview of November 17, 1980.
4. Interview of Commander T. A. Christopher, USN. OpNav-16-V-E 192 dated September 15, 1944.

5. Vadm V. Utgoff, December 29, 1943 to January 13, 1945, unpublished.
6. Patrol Squadron 34 Aircraft Action Report #12. Date of Action January 11, 1944.
7. Christopher interview of September 15, 1944.
8. Christopher interview of September 15, 1944.
9. Christopher interview of September 15, 1944.
10. Patrol Squadron 34 Aircraft Action Report #15. Date of Action January 15, 1944.

11. Christopher interview of September 15, 1944.
12. Carroll R. Anderson, "Mission to Kavieng," *American Aviation Historical Society Journal*, Summer 1965, pp. 88-101.

13. CoSoPac to ComSeventh Flt 170006—2 February 1944.

Chapter 12

1. U.S.S. *San Pablo*, Ship's Memorandum No. 1-44 dated March 24, 1944 promulgated Senior Officer Present Afloat, Admiralty Islands Area, Order No. 1 of March 13, 1944.

2. *San Pablo* Memorandum of March 24, 1944.
3. Letter from Captain Jules M. Busker, USNR (Ret.), dated November 28, 1980.
4. Busker letter of November 28, 1980.

5. Busker letter of November 28, 1980.

6. A. O. Van Wyen, *The Development of Fleet Air Wings*, Deputy Chief of Naval Operations (Air) 1946, p. 747.

7. Commander Aircraft Seventh Fleet Memorandum, Subject: Black Cat Operations, Serial 0515 of September 29, 1944.

8. Utgoff and Day, "The Cat's Tale." A series of articles appearing in *Shipmate* magazine from February through November 1946.

9. Letter from Howard R. Kenyon, undated.

10. Patrol Squadron 33 Aircraft Action Report A-7, Date of Action September 5, 1944.

11. Patrol Squadron 33 Aircraft Action Report A-12. Date of Action September 16, 1944.

12. Patrol Squadron 33 Aircraft Action Report A-17. Date of Action September 23, 1944.

13. Letter from Captain Fernald P. Anderson, USN (Ret.), dated April 26, 1981.

14. Letter from William B. Sumpter of December 18, 1980. See also *Air Op Memo*, Commander Air Force Pacific Fleet of March 26, 1945, pp. 16, 17.

15. Commander Seventh Fleet to Commander Aircraft Seventh Fleet of October 5, 1944—Retransmittal of MacArthur message.

Chapter 13

1. Interview with Commander James F. Merritt, USN (Ret.) of May 3, 1981.

2. Interview with Lieutenant Commander Vadm V. Utgoff, USN dated October 10, 1945.

3. Letter from Captain L. R. Heron, USN (Ret.) of February 26, 1981.

4. Heron letter of February 26, 1981.

5. Utgoff interview of October 10, 1945.

Index

Library of Congress Cataloging in Publication Data

Knott, Richard C.
  Black Cat Raiders of World War II.

  Includes bibliographical reference and index.
  1. World War, 1939-1945 – Aerial operations,
American. 2. World War, 1939-1945 – Pacific Ocean.
3. United States. Army Air Forces – History – World
War, 1939-1945. I. Title.
D790.K58   940.54'4973   81-11352
ISBN 0-955852-18-5   AACR2

198